Triathlon Disasters
& How to Avoid Them

Paul N. Bloom and David K. Williams

Illustrations by John Holladay

DEDICATION

We dedicate this book to our families who have had to suffer through the embarrassment and worry that we've put you through with our mishaps, and to all our friends, family members, and clients who have persevered through their own triathlon disasters and gone on to finish countless other races!

CONTENTS

ACKNOWLEDGMENTS

Our wives, Shelly Bloom and Monette Williams – our partners in life as well as in triathlon coaching and training – provided several of the stories in this book and offered great support for this writing endeavor. We also appreciate the creative genius of John Holladay of Martha's Vineyard, MA, who contributed the cartoons and cover art.

1 – INTRODUCTION

Speed Bump

Somebody yelled at me as I took off on the bike leg of one of my first triathlons, but I couldn't hear the words through my water-clogged ears and heavy breathing. Turns out it was "Watch the speed bump!" and I ended up hitting it at full speed, getting thrown over the handle bars onto my head and shoulders. I was so stunned and disoriented that I jumped back on the bike thinking I could tough it out and finish the race. But 10 seconds later I hit another speed bump that I didn't see and got thrown again onto the hard pavement. My clavicle was broken and I was torn to shreds. I ended up in the emergency room of the hospital where my mother had just died a few weeks before. What a disaster! P.B.

Murphy's Law – *if anything can go wrong, it will* – clearly applies to triathlon. One of the unique aspects about triathlon is that it's nearly impossible to have the perfect race due to there being such a plethora of pieces that all have to come together, more so than almost any other sport. That's one factor that makes this sport great; you can always find ways to improve. In our many years of racing and coaching, we have personally experienced and witnessed an incredible array of "disasters" and other experiences – some of which you would never anticipate – that have left athletes aggravated, disappointed, second-guessing themselves, amazed, and amused. As we're sure many of you reading this can relate to, we have seen forgotten helmets, shoes, goggles, bicycles, and wetsuits, all kinds of wrong turns, equipment failures of uniforms and bikes, crashes and spinouts, surprise weather events, urgent calls of nature nowhere near a porta-potty or bathroom, awful muscle cramping and bonking, and visits to hospitals because of accidents, hypothermia, dehydration, hypernatremia, or elevated heart rates. You name it, we've likely witnessed it, if not done it ourselves. Even the most experienced athletes and coaches make the craziest of blunders, which we can all learn from.

In more than a few cases, we have seen disasters persuade novice triathletes to give up the sport and never race again. In most situations, though, people do bounce back from these missteps, trying to learn from their mistakes so that they can do better the next time. Often, of course, some new unanticipated event awaits them at their next race. However, gradually the number of disasters tends to dissipate and become less severe, so that more uneventful and successful racing occurs. While we, unfortunately, haven't found a way to totally eliminate disasters and mishaps in our own races or our clients' races, as you will see, we have learned to minimize and manage them through application of what we have labeled the PREPARE approach. PREPARE is an acronym for:

> **Plan**: Think through every single aspect of the race, from packing and pre-race travel to post-race cool-down and recovery. Visualize how different actions will work for you and commit to taking those actions that you think will work best. Good luck follows the prepared.

> **Rehearse**: It really helps to simulate or test race experiences before you are actually in the midst of a race. From laying out your transition space to testing the water conditions to practicing bicycle mounting and dismounting to eating while riding and running, the more you have tried and practiced them, the better off you'll be at race time. The obverse of this advice is even more important: *Never try anything brand new during a race!*

Execute: Sticking to the plan. Don't change your mind about how to do something at the last minute or on the spur of the moment – *unless* an unusual or unexpected race situation requires you to think fast and adapt to this situation. Having Plan Bs or contingency plans ready to go when unexpected or unwanted things occur is vitally important, such as planning on how to deal with a flat tire during a race.

Persist: Don't let deviations from the plan, no matter what the cause, throw you for a loop. If something happens that costs you significant time, just become determined to make up the time *gradually* later in the race. Or just enjoy the bliss of being able to do this wonderful sport and soak everything in. Most importantly, don't get frustrated and give up.

Analyze: Always conduct a post-race analysis, especially when a mistake or disaster occurs, so that you can determine why it happened and figure out how it can be avoided or how you could limit its impact in the future. Get advice from a coach or knowledgeable friend on how to deal more effectively with similar incidents.

Revise: Take the plan, or parts of the plan, that went wrong and modify it before using it in another race with similar distances and conditions. Take account of what you learned from your analysis. The best athletes never stop learning and adapting.

Enjoy: Don't beat yourself up and keep obsessing about mistakes. No matter what, keep triathlon fun! – something that keeps a smile on your face and gives you loads of pleasure through helping you feel fit, healthy, and enjoying the camaraderie of other multisport athletes. Get pleasure out of the sights, scenery, and locations where you race. Don't get too serious about it or you'll burn out.

In this book, we want to alert you to our experiences with

the many different disasters and challenges that can confront you in a triathlon, showing you how applying our PREPARE approach can either prevent these disasters or mitigate their effects. You'll have fun reflecting on your own personal stories and experiences as you laugh, cringe, and cry along with us. We hope what we say here will resonate with you no matter what type of triathlete you are. Whether you do sprint-distance races (typically around 750 meter swim, 12.4 mile or 20K bike, and 3.1 mile or 5K run), ironman-distance races (2.4 mile swim, 112 mile bike, and 26.2 mile run), or any other distances or disciplines, and whether you are a novice triathlete or an experienced old-hand, we have stories to tell to peak your interest and make you laugh, as well as advice to give that will make your triathlon racing experiences less stressful and more rewarding. Our goal is to help make it possible for you to enjoy competing in triathlons well into your senior years, benefitting from the tremendous things the sport can do for your physical, mental, and emotional well-being.

We decided that the most logical way to present our ideas is to have separate chapters on each portion of a typical triathlon. Thus, we have chapters on:

- Pre-race travel and set-up

- Swimming

- T1 (transition from swim to bike)

- Biking

- T2 (transition from bike to run)

- Running

- Post-race cool-down and recovery

Each chapter will open with a few entertaining stories, highlighting where things went terribly wrong for one of us or for someone we know during that portion of a race. We have signed our own stories with our initials, but there are several embarrassing stories that we report with identities that have been kept confidential. So you will read about disasters such as forgotten equipment at set-up, wrong turns in swims, broken wetsuit zippers that wouldn't unzip in T1, bike crashes and flat tires, penalties in T2 for removing a bike helmet too soon, a leg that snapped in half during a run, and painful post-race cramping that caused a scary fall down steps upon returning to a hotel. Some of our stories will overlap more than a single topic, in which case we've put them where they seemed most appropriate or in a supplementary chapter at the end with 'bonus stories'. In each chapter, we will discuss how employing the PREPARE approach during that race portion might have allowed the avoidance of those disasters or, at a minimum, made them less disruptive and upsetting. And we also supply other pertinent advice. Of course, we can't give you a formula for totally eliminating disasters, but we think we can help you reduce their frequency, intensity, and impact.

2 – PRE-RACE TRAVEL AND SET-UP

We can laugh about the following stories now, but they caused enough stress at the time to last a while. Ever make mistakes that cost you a lot of time or that put you in the doghouse? Uh huh, so have we!

Taking the Back Roads

Several years ago, I was doing an internship at Virginia Tech University and had talked a friend into doing a small triathlon in West Virginia over a free weekend as a fun challenge. I had done the race before and really enjoyed it. It had good open water, nice hills, good scenery, great post-race food, and incredible prizes. As you can imagine, we were pumped for the race! While I had been there previously, I had come from a totally different direction so was unfamiliar with the route we would have to take. The website didn't have directions on it so, naturally, we used Mapquest or something similar (this was before GPS units and cellphones provided directions).

We thought it would take about 1 1/2 hours of driving to get to the venue. We wanted to arrive early enough to get set-up and get in a good warm-up so we left between 2 1/2 to 3 hours to get there and get everything ready. The first 45-60 minutes went smoothly and according to plan. As we got further into West Virginia, though, the roads kept getting narrower, steeper, and less populated. We started to get a bit nervous, but I knew that the race was in a sparsely populated area so I wasn't too worried . . . yet! That is, until the street crossings started to not have street signs and the roads became gravel. The directions had us making quick turns that didn't match up with distances on the roads and without street signs we were, yes I admit it, lost. The roads actually became pure dirt, there was absolutely no one around, and we didn't feel comfortable knocking on the doors of the rare house or trailer that we saw.

After driving around taking random roads and much backtracking, we finally got to a road that I recognized and we got to the race site about 10-minutes before the race start. Luckily it was a smaller race, because we managed to park, get set up, and run into the water just as the race started. The stress of the drive must have done something, though, because I ended up having a great race, taking the win with my best 10k triathlon run on a hilly course.

Following the race I asked my friend how he got the directions. It ends up that he had clicked on the 'most direct' route thinking that would be the best option. Poor choice! D.W.

Tip One: Leave enough time to drive to the race site accounting for the possibility of unforeseen delays. You never know what may come up!

Don't Trust Your Spouse

We were doing a fun sprint-distance race at the beach in North Carolina, which started with a half-mile ocean swim and then had two six-mile out-and-back loops of a bike course, followed by a 5K run. My wife, Shelly, started in a wave 5 minutes behind me, and since she is a slightly faster swimmer than I and much faster on transitions, I figured I would see her trailing me by only about 3 minutes on the bike course. Sure enough, at exactly 1 and one-half minutes after I did the first turn-around on the bike loop, we passed each other going in opposite directions, urging each other on.

That was the last time I saw her during the race. On my second loop of the bike course, I noticed that there was some commotion around someone who had crashed at the turn-around, but I didn't see that it was Shelly. As I waited at the finish line after completing my race, I got pretty worried when I didn't see her come in, as expected, only a few minutes behind me. The fact that I had not seen Shelly on the second bike loop added to my concern. Indeed, it took about a half hour before Shelly hobbled in, all bloody and bruised from having been the person in that crash. (She still finished second in her age group!)

What went wrong? This one, of course, was my fault. The race we had done prior to this one required us to ship our bikes in a large two-bike box that we use. To get the bikes in that box, we have to take off the pedals (as well as disassemble other parts). In getting ready for this beach race, I volunteered to re-assemble our bikes, so that Shelly could tend to other things. However, in putting on her pedals, I didn't tighten one of them properly. Hence, when Shelly hit that first turn-around, putting all her weight on the outside pedal to accelerate, the pedal snapped off and she went flying over her handlebars. Banged up and stunned, she waited for the EMC people to show up for over 20 minutes, and when they did, they had no ice – and they also tried to get her to quit the race. By this time, she had no patience with them and insisted on getting back on the bike to finish. Luckily, she had done enough 1-pedal cycling drills to make finishing the bike on 1 pedal possible. Fortunately, there were no broken bones or long-lasting injuries to recover from, but as you can imagine, she was furious with me!

Ever since then we take complete responsibility for disassembling and assembling our own bikes before races. P.B.

Tip Two: Make sure your equipment is in good working order.

Pre-race travel and set-up presents the potential for all kinds of issues and disasters. Problems can emerge because of oversights, unexpected events, and bad choices during:

- Packing

- Traveling

- Sleeping

- Eating and Drinking

- Dealing with bathroom needs

- Preparing gear and equipment

- Warming up your body and final prep

Just to name a handful. Here are a few stories and solutions under each of these headings. We follow them with advice about how the PREPARE approach could have prevented these incidents.

Packing

Forgotten Saddle

We were down in St.Croix, where I was planning to do the half-ironman (70.3) and my wife was going to do the sprint race. We opened our bike box to start to assemble our bikes and Shelly's seat post and saddle were not there. She had left them at home on the floor next to where we packed the bikes. Fortunately, the local bike shop was able to lend us a post/saddle for the race, which was very uncomfortable and created a few saddle sores, but she was still able to do the race (and get fourth place overall among women). P.B.

Tip Three: Be sure you've packed everything...and that you know how to pack it all. Or, if you do forget something, it helps to have someone willing to make a quick trip.

Forgotten Bike Box

This is a truly embarrassing and painful story, but some of you will

10

get a laugh out of it and a few may actually sympathize with me and/or learn something. The first year that I signed up to race at the national championships, in 1998, I was young and had never traveled by air to a race before. In fact, I had only flown a couple of times ever at that point, and never where I was handling any of the details myself. I had just graduated from college and was going with my girlfriend, Monette, (now my wife) to stay with her sister who lived near the race in Orlando, FL.

So, I can't even imagine what the ticket counter attendants were thinking when this young guy comes up wheeling his FULLY ASSEMBLED bike. I had absolutely no idea that you were supposed to box your bike! They were nice enough to tell me what I needed to do and even had a cardboard bike box that I could try to use if I could get it together in time. Of course, I had never taken my bike apart before, let alone try to pack it into a box. I tried my best, shoved everything into the box, and taped it shut. Yes, this is my tri-bike that I'm talking about! I brought it up to the counter as they were making last-calls, but they refused to accept the bike for travel because the box wouldn't close properly. Not wanting to waste our tickets for Orlando, though, we somehow talked the agent into keeping the bike behind the counter until I had someone pick it up. So, I called a friend to make the pick-up and luckily got ahold of him while we were running through the airport. He was nice enough to help us out by going to the airport to get the bike, which I'm sure you probably wouldn't be able to do these days. We just made it in time for take-off.

In Orlando, I picked up my race packet and enjoyed the pre-race expo. But, after that, we made the most of the weekend by going to Disney World and Universal Studios. Of course, to this day my brother-in-law still teases me about not bringing my bike to a national championship race! D.W.

I Owe You One, Sis!

A few years ago, USA Triathlon had its Age-Group Sprint-Distance National Championships in Ithaca, New York, where Shelly's sister lives. So we entered the race and made a family weekend out of it, having a great time visiting our two young nieces (about 5 at the time) and their parents.

While packing up the night before the race, Shelly spent most of her time explaining to everyone where they should stand during the race – so that we could benefit from hearing their cheers at multiple points on the course. With her attention focused elsewhere, she forgot to pack her biking shoes in the bags she was taking to the race site. Thus, when she arrived at the transition area on race morning, she realized she only had her running shoes and the flip flops on her feet. And her sister's house was over 20 minutes away – too far for us to drive back, get the shoes, return to the race site, park, and make the race start time.

Thankfully, we had a cell phone with us and we were able to call Shelly's sister to get her to bring the shoes. Having lived in that area for many years, she knew exactly which roads to take and where to meet Shelly to make her delivery in the nick of time. And somehow, she was also able to get her daughters out the door fast enough to make the delivery with her. They all had a great time cheering us on, and Shelly even went on to win her age group!
P.B.

The following story has several good elements to it, including why you shouldn't just blindly follow someone when drafting in open water. However, the story goes well with the line of advice in this chapter on pre race preparations.

Forgotten Goggles

It had been a very long season, so I thought I would back out of a half ironman race that I had registered for several months earlier. It was reasonably close by, so the morning of the race, I decided that I'd go to the race with my bike to cheer on several friends who were racing that morning. But I took some stuff with me, just in case I changed my mind, as I had picked up my packet the day before. Of course, I got to the race site and the weather was beautiful, the atmosphere was fun, and the athletes all looked ready to roll. Wow, why would I not just do the race and have fun with it without putting any pressure on myself?

I started getting ready and realized that I really wasn't prepared to race. I didn't have a lot of things, one of which was swim goggles! I quickly asked around and the only one who had something to offer on such short notice was one of my biggest competitors. How old the goggles were, I have no idea, but they were far from new. In fact, the straps were rotting!

By now, you should not be surprised to hear that the strap broke after just a few strokes into the race. I'm not a big fan of swimming without goggles, but I managed okay on the way out from the start. However, the path back in had us swimming directly into the rising sun and I couldn't see a thing! I swam so far off course that I actually ran into shore instead of swimming parallel to it. Yikes! But, what happened next really shocked me. My friend who gave me the goggles literally swam right into my back!! He had just blindly followed me without ever bothering to see if we were on track. I couldn't stop laughing at what that had to look like throughout the rest of the swim. In spite of all this, I ended up finishing just about a minute ahead of my friend for third place. If he hadn't followed me into shore... who knows? D.W.

Tip Four: Have back-up goggles, race belts, and anything else that can be easily broken or lost. If you do need something, sometimes your direct competitors aren't the ones to borrow forgotten items from.

We could go on and on with stories of forgotten uniforms, bike shoes, helmets, race belts, sunscreens, Body Glide, bike wheels, and sunglasses. Needless to say, a good packing checklist (see Exhibit 1) can help avoid these oversights and forgetful moments. But in addition to following a checklist, it is valuable to pay attention to what the weather conditions and course challenges will be. If there is a chance that the water or air temperature will be really cold, then you may want to pack an extra compression-type top that you can wear under your uniform (and wetsuit) to keep you warmer. Socks, gloves, jackets, chemical hand or foot warmers, and headbands might also be appropriate.

****

Exhibit 1

Packing Check List

Swim:

- o **Goggles (2)**
- o **Cap**
- o **Ear plugs**
- o **Body Glide or other lubricant**
- o **SpeedSuit and/or Wetsuit**
- o **Neoprene cap and booties if warranted**
- o **Swimsuit**
- o **Timing chip**
- o **Timing chip strap**

T1/Bike:

- o **Towel**
- o **Cycling shoes**
- o **Helmet**
- o **Bike**
- o **Water bottles**
- o **Aero bottle**
- o **Race nutrition**
- o **Sunglasses**
- o **Spare tube**
- o **CO_2 cartridge and attachment**
- o **Tire Levers/tools**
- o **Chain Lube**
- o **Floor Pump**
- o **Race Wheels**
- o **Socks**

T2/Run:

- o **Race Belt**
- o **Race Number**
- o **Hat**
- o **Running Shoes**

Miscellaneous:

o **Flip flops/Sandals**
o **Pre- and post-race clothes**
o **Rain/wind jacket**
o **Toilet paper**
o **Course maps**
o **Head light**
o **Sun block**
o **USAT Card**
o **Drivers license**
o **Watch/Garmin**

****

A great tip one of us had during one race, which was surprisingly cold and windy, was to use plastic grocery bags under a jersey. Newspapers, which are popular among cyclists, don't work well if wet, which is inevitable in a triathlon, but the plastic works great. That tip got Dave through one of his Ironman races. After doing a race where you can't put on your shoes because your fingers don't work and your feet feel like bricks, you'll quickly learn that dressing appropriately is vital!

If hot weather is possible, think of clothing that will keep you cooler, as well as other equipment that might help in keeping your temperature down. At one particular race, the water was cold enough that a wetsuit was a must, but the air temperature created an unusually hot day. Dave had to get in his wetsuit before getting corralled and was sweating so badly that people asked him about his swim warm up! It would have been smarter in that case to wait as long as humanly possible before putting on the wetsuit because he lost a lot of water through sweat before even starting the race.

Toe covers, ear warmers, sunglasses, and knowing where to put ice can make the difference between finishing strong and comfortable or succumbing to the weather. In hot and humid races, putting ice or, at least, cold water on your groin, chest, and in your hands helps to keep your core temperature down.

Keep Cool

It really has helped me to have places to put ice during hot races. Wearing a cap instead of a visor to hold ice on my head, wearing a wristband to hold ice against my wrist, and shoving ice into my compression shorts have all provided some relief. For a race in Monterrey, Mexico that my wife once did in 105 degree heat, she froze a set of ice packs in the hotel kitchen the night before the race and then taped them to her upper body and head on race morning as a way to cool her body down before the start. It worked, she won her age group! P.B.

And if you think the bike course might have steeper hills than indicated on the race web site and you have the option, you might want to bring an extra cassette or a rear wheel with a cassette that has easier gearing. Or if you think you will be staring into the sun during the swim, make sure to bring dark goggles that will shade some of the light.

Tip Five: Be prepared for the elements.

<u>Traveling</u>

Flipping Bikes

You've probably heard the horror stories, but I've personally known two different instances of people losing the bikes from their cars. The first time, I was following behind a couple of friends on the way to a race. Their bikes were both on top of the car with the front forks locked into the rack. Unfortunately for one of them, who happened to be a pro triathlete, his fork wasn't fully secured. I watched, horrified, as the bike flipped backwards and hung onto the car with a strap on the rear wheel. Unbelievably, the bike was mostly okay, but, sadly, he ruined a new rear aero wheel. He was lucky and did compete in the race on a borrowed wheel. The second time was a client of mine who carpooled with a friend for a drive to age group nationals in Vermont. Her bike fell off early in the drive and after getting it checked out in Burlington, the day before the race mind you, realized it needed a lot of work including

a new fork. Amazingly, she got things rigged ~~e~~
do the race, but to finish top five females overall
fun way to spend the 24 hours before a big race.

Tip Six: Make sure your bike is well sec

Presidential Welcome

*I had spent hours figuring out the logistics for a trip to France,
where I was going to race in the Age-Group Duathlon (10K run,
40K bike, 5K run) World Championships in the charming city of
Nancy. I planned to fly from Raleigh, NC to JFK Airport in New
York on a Thursday afternoon, transfer to a flight to Paris that
evening, arrive in Paris the following morning, take a high-speed
train to Nancy from the Paris airport, and then go pick up my race
packet, reassemble my bike, and rest for the remainder of the day
on Friday. The next day, Saturday, would be used to check out the
course and transitions, as well to as rack my bike and rest up for
the early start on Sunday.*

*But President Obama screwed all this up for me. It turns out that
he was flying out of JFK around the same time I was arriving, and
for security reasons they made my plane sit on the tarmac for 2
hours before they allowed us to deplane into the terminal. That
was just long enough to have me miss my flight to Paris, and the
next flight they could put me on was the same one the following
day. So I ended up arriving on Saturday, after packet pick-up was
over and with little time to reassemble my bike, learn the course
logistics, and rack my bike, let alone get some rest. With the help
of the Team USA support crew, who picked up my packet for me
and showed me the ropes, I got it all together and had a good race.
But how well would I have done if President Obama had left JFK a
few minutes earlier? P.B.*

International Incidents

*I've had numerous funny (now!) things happen when traveling to
various races. I was once stopped and pulled out of the customs
line by a security officer in Australia. He had my bag pulled aside*

...asked me to confirm that it was mine. I said yes, and he then asked me to follow him. I went to a side room where he started asking me a bunch of questions before making me unload my bag. It turns out that the bomb-sniffing dog had somehow targeted my bag! After answering a million questions and convincing them that I didn't have, or hadn't handled, any bomb materials, they came to the conclusion that the grease that was used on my pedals, which were in my bag on that trip to save weight in the bike box, set the dog off.

Another time, I was an assistant coach for the US team at an ITU World Cup race in South Korea. At their airport they have military guards walking around with machine guns over their shoulders. I didn't know whether that should make me feel safer or not! But, as we were at the counter a Korean woman started going crazy and yelling at the top of her voice. We had no clue what she was saying, but we started to get concerned when the guards picked up their guns and started running her way. Then, to our surprise, she looks back and decides to jump over the counter, onto the conveyor belt and rides it into the back!! The guards quickly caught up to her and pulled her out before dragging her away. I haven't the slightest idea of what was being said or what happened, but it was quite scary. D.W.

Adrenaline At Its Best

Again, always leave plenty of extra time for traffic when staying a good distance away from a race. My wife and I thought that we had done that when staying at a sister-in-law's house an hour away from the race one year at the Eagleman Triathlon on the Eastern Shore of Maryland. We left with enough time to get there at least an hour and a half prior to the start, and since we had already picked up our packets, applied our numbers, and scoped everything out that should have been plenty of time... right? Not so much.

We were heading over a bridge and just as we were almost past it, we noticed that there had been an accident and traffic had stopped with about four cars or so in front of us. It was very tragic. We *didn't know it right away, but the car caught on fire with people still trapped inside. It was very early in the morning and we were stopped on the bridge for hours as the police and ambulances showed up and did their thing. There was nothing we could do and we were okay with that, because it was out of our control, although I had really been looking forward to racing. Of course, the worst part was that we had hydrated well for the race and were both more than desperate for relief. Yes, we ended up using the doors and towels for a little bit of privacy as we peed on the side of the bridge, as did the other triathletes and fishermen that were stuck along with us!*

When the traffic was finally allowed to move, I saw that there was no way that we were going to get to the race in time for the start. However, Tim DeBoom and Natascha Badmann, both reigning Ironman champions, were supposed to race so we decided to go to the race as spectators and enjoy the day. We parked in the lot and as we were getting out of the car I could hear the announcer saying "If you were stuck in the traffic jam and just arrived, you can still race if you can make it in the water for our last wave. We will let you start with the relay wave." Wow, that's awesome! Uh oh, that's less than 10 minutes from now!

We grabbed our bikes and sprinted to the transition area. Somehow, I managed to throw all of my stuff that I needed onto the ground, as did my wife, and we sprinted to the beach. I was getting into the water as the wave was already lined up, only to realize that in my haste I had started to put my wetsuit on backwards! UGHH. Off and on it goes again. It's not pulled up right, but I'm out of time. The gun sounds and I just go. You want to talk about adrenaline! I swam my way through what felt like 1000 people having started behind the last wave.

After exiting the water, I grabbed my bike and took off out of transition. I reached for my bottle to swish out my mouth only to realize that I had forgotten to put any of my nutrition on my bike! Luckily, they had aid stations every 10-15 miles that were at least handing out water. I got to the first aid station and, as luck would have it, the kid that was handing me the water bottle didn't want to let go. I caught my balance, but the bottle dropped to the ground and I couldn't stop to get it with hundreds of people on the course around me. So, at this point, I realized that I'm going to be going about 1 1/2 hours at least without any liquid or nutrition and that's most likely going to catch up to me at some point. With that in mind, and with youthful exuberance, I decided to just go for broke. I pushed down on my pedals determined to go hard and find my limits.

Interestingly, I ended up finishing the swim and bike with roughly the same splits as Tim DeBoom - and that's with having to navigate through everybody! On the run, I did the first seven miles right at a 6:00 average pace, which was really good for me at the time. However, sorry folks, but there's no great 'and I won the race anyway' finish to this story. That's when the wall hit, and it hit hard! I walked/jogged the rest of the run, getting whatever I could muster out of my legs. However, I had gone fast enough in the swim and bike, and the start of the run, so that I still finished in the top 20 overall including pros, as well as 2nd in my age group. I learned a lot that day! My wife had a very good finish as well. Not too bad considering that just over 4 hours earlier we were planning on watching from the sidelines! D.W.

Tip Seven: Be prepared to get set up quickly if something does delay your travels.

Besides flight delays and traffic accidents, we have had our pre-race travel plans spoiled by poor directions (see this chapter's opening story), lost baggage (including our bikes – several times), broken bike carriers, and forgotten picture IDs (to get through airport security – and also packet pick-up). These kinds of unexpected events can disturb your pre-race routine, making it harder for you to get the nutrition, rest, equipment preparation, course scouting, and warm-up you need to perform your best. There is no simple way to avoid these hassles. Some people find it useful to work through travel agents when going to races that involve air travel, hotels, and the like. Indeed, there are several agents that specialize in helping triathletes with their travel arrangements (see Exhibit 2). For some time-pressured athletes, the time savings and peace of mind an agent can provide are clearly worth the extra fees that are usually charged.

∎∎

Exhibit 2

Travel Agents for Triathlon

Endurance Sports Travel
www.endurancesportstravel.com
info@endurancesportstravel.com 610-399-4662

Premium Plus Sports
www.premiumplus-sports.com
info@premiumplus-sports.com   800-282-3636

Tri the World Travel
www.tritheworld.com
infor@tritheworld.com   202-468-0265

∎∎

Our advice is to stay calm and collected, being mentally prepared for things to go wrong. We've actually gotten to the point where we think that our bikes not making it on our flight is a good thing because then the airlines deliver the bikes directly to your hotel, room, or wherever you're staying, rather than requiring you to lug it around yourself! Also, moving your pre-race warm-ups around is not going to make a difference on race day no matter how much you think you're wedded to your schedule!

Cutting it Close!

As Monette and I were packing the day before leaving for the World Championships in Hamburg, Germany, I casually asked Monette to check our passports to make sure we packed them. Luckily, she looked at them and made a comment that her's expired in a few weeks. UH OH! Your passport has to be valid for several months after the visit! It was in the afternoon and we were to leave on an early morning flight out of RDU. We immediately got on the Internet and started making calls. Finally, Monette was told that the only way to get a passport that quickly and have any chance of making it on the trip was to be first in line at the office in Washington D.C. the next morning, pay an extra fee, and hope that they could get it done quickly. That obviously wouldn't work to make our flight out of RDU. UGH.

BUT, our connecting flight was out of Philadelphia, drivable from Washington D.C.. We decided to chance it. Monette got maybe an hour of sleep or so, then left around 3am to drive to D.C. Luckily, she had a sister who lived near there and met her there for support and some coffee/food. She waited in line for a long time, but managed to get in front of the line.

Meanwhile, I have to start my trip not knowing how things are going. I board the plane to Philadelphia worried about how Monette is dealing with everything. After I land, I call her and find out that she managed to get the passport and was on her way to Philadelphia. Time was still tight and we had to hope for no traffic issues. But, by some miracle, she made it to the airport in time and was able to check in and enjoy the rest of the trip. I still have no idea how the stars aligned to be able to pull that one off, but it's a mistake that we will surely never make again! D.W.

Whether you need to fly to your destination or not, in general, the sooner you can get to the race venue before the race, the better. Yes, it may cost more money for an extra night at a hotel to come a day earlier, but the cushion this can provide you for dealing with unplanned surprises may pay dividends in how you perform in the race. This is especially the case if you are traveling to a location where the climate and conditions are different from what you are used to. Getting your body acclimated to extremes of heat or cold, wind, altitude, or humidity, including very cold water temperature, can be very helpful. This can sometimes mean arriving several days early, not just one or two. An example is acclimating to heat, as it takes about five days to start to adjust and two weeks to fully acclimate. For this case, it's best to get out and exercise in the heat for about an hour per day starting out easy during the first few days.

Extreme Heat

I flew into Las Vegas on a Friday night in order to compete in the Age-Group 70.3 World Championships that were being held there on that Sunday morning. It was early September and the temperature was going well over 100 every day, much hotter than I had been experiencing in North Carolina. A good part of Saturday was spent in air conditioning getting my bike ready, registering, and eating, so I really didn't get a chance to experience the extreme heat, let alone acclimate to it. On race day, I felt fine during the swim and bike, but when I started the run, my body and head got so hot that it scared me. Not only that, they ran out of ice! So I decided to drop out after one loop (4.3 miles) of a 3 loop run. I didn't even want to try to walk the rest of the race. On the bus back to the race start, where my car was parked, we passed a thermometer that said 110. I'm not sure what would have happened had I acclimated more, but certainly the way I tried to do it didn't work. P.B.

Tip Eight: Allow time to acclimatize, if possible.

Sleeping

Pre-Race Nap

We've all been there. You just can't sleep prior to a race and show up groggy and bleary-eyed. That's usually okay as the sleep the night before doesn't really affect your race, believe it or not. However, if you didn't get enough sleep two and/or three days prior to the race, you'll likely feel it. A friend of mine can testify to just how rough race morning can sometimes be when absolutely exhausted.

Like most athletes, he had to use the porta-john prior to the race and managed to get in one shortly, but with plenty of time, before the start of the race. However, he was startled when he heard the gun go off! What happened? You may have guessed it; he actually had fallen asleep in the porta-john! The good part of the story is that he was still able to get out and do the race, just with a little bit of a late start. D.W.

Sleepless in Charlotte

For races in the Charlotte, NC area, we always drive down the day before (for 2.5 hours), pick up our packets, have an early dinner, and try to get a good night sleep before getting up at around 5am to get to the race venue for a 7 or 8am start. For this one sprint race, we decided to stay at a hotel that was a race sponsor, a few miles from the race site. All was well except that at about 2:30 am the fire alarm went off and over 200 triathletes, in an incredible array of sleeping apparel, ended up milling around the parking lot for a half hour, waiting for the alarm to stop (and also probably scouting which of their competitors were there and which weren't). I know I never got back to sleep that night and I'm sure it affected my performance. P.B.

Tip Nine: The most important night of sleep is two nights before the race, not necessarily the night before.

People vary enormously in their need for sleep and in their ability to fall asleep in noisy or uncomfortable situations. Some people can sleep on airplanes, some cannot. Some need a special pillow to avoid waking up with a stiff neck, others can sleep on a rock and feel just fine in the morning. You can now wear simple monitors that will tell you how much sleep you get and what kind of quality that sleep was. It may surprise you to see the data, which can, obviously, be very useful!

Ear Plugs to the Rescue

One of my best buddies offered to share a room with me to help defray the expenses of an especially expensive race in a resort area – my wife couldn't make this trip. I was grateful for the savings and the company, until I realized that my friend was a very loud snorer, even louder than the noisy air conditioner in the

room. Thankfully, I had brought ear plugs with me and they muffled most of the sounds, allowing me to get decent amounts of sleep the nights before the race. P.B.

Tip Ten: Bring ear plugs to combat loud streets, air conditioners, neighbors, snorers, etc.

Going into a race sleep-deprived and tired is generally not optimal, even though the adrenaline rush you can get from racing can often compensate for the lack of sleep. Thus, you should do what you can to facilitate getting a good night's sleep for several nights before a big race. If that means using ear plugs, special pillows, blindfolds, soothing music, a warm glass of milk, or anything else, then remember to bring these necessities on your trip. One of us needs to read a book to fall asleep quickly, and if he forgets bedtime reading it takes him significantly longer to drift off. Also remember to bring something that will wake you up on time. If the night before a race you don't sleep very much – because of pre-race jitters, unfamiliar surroundings, uncomfortable beds, a fire alarm, or noisy (and snoring) neighbors – don't worry, since your muscles will still be resting as long as you aren't pacing the floor. But make sure you get some quality sleep, even if it's done in naps, in the days before a race.

Busted

There is a popular race venue in North Carolina that is only a bit under two hours away. But, it's nice to still be able to sleep in a little later and stay close to the race site. The options for this race are pretty limited. You can stay at cabins on site, which I have done on a couple of occasions, but I still find it hard to get a good night's sleep because it's open air and can be noisy, or you can stay at a hotel about a half hour away. We chose the latter option one year. A good plan, but not one that went the way we hoped. As we hopped into bed the party next door was just getting started. The noise ramped up, got very rowdy, and then fights broke out. It got so bad that we were trying to stay away from the windows. The cops eventually came out to break things up and ended up busting several of the people for drugs. Our night of full sleep turned into a stressful one with only a few hours of rest! D.W.

Eating and Drinking

Too Much of a Good Thing

Anyone that knows me will tell you that I love to eat, and, being in North Carolina, there's not much better than pulled pork barbecue. So, I was in heaven when I found out that there were two, yes, two, parties offering pulled pork on the same day, one of which was an actual pig-pickin' where the meat is taken fresh off of the pig. I don't know how much I ate, but it was a lot and it was good! Of course, that may not have been the best idea the night before the race but I figured I'd be fine. Oh, how wrong I was.

The race started off well and I was first out of the water and off of the bike. However, I soon realized that something was wrong as I got into the run. My legs were stiff and I started cramping, something I had never experienced before. It continued to get worse, but I managed to struggle through to the finish in second place. Shortly after the finish, though, to put it as nicely as possible, I began having a lot of blood coming out of both ends. We didn't stay for awards, deciding instead to head for emergency care. The ride was memorable, and not in a good way. My gut had me doubled over and cringing in pain. To make a long story short, I ended up having e-coli poisoning, which made for an interesting and miserably unpleasant few days, but a lasting triathlon race story. D.W.

While it is always important for triathletes to be vigilant about what they are putting in their bodies, it is especially important to be careful about nutrition in the days and hours leading up to a race. You want to be well-fueled and hydrated when a race starts, but you don't want to feel stuffed, sluggish, gassy, nauseous, or needing to go to the bathroom when the gun goes off. Many endurance athletes still carbo-load with pasta the night or two before a race. But that philosophy has been abandoned by many of the athletes we know, and they generally prefer to eat a light, balanced meal with some protein for satiety (e.g., fish, chicken, tofu) and carbs the night prior to a race. What works better for most people who like to carbo load is to increase carbs slightly the week of the race and with the main carb meal two nights before the race. However, you don't want to just have carbs or you'll feel bloated and sluggish while likely overeating. Having a bit of fat and protein will help with satiety and have you feeling and performing better. If it's going to be a hot race, it can also help to add a bit more salt to your meals than you normally do during that week leading up to it. Also, hydrate well during the days before a race, and, again, try to make sure that you have an ample amount of sodium during that time period (especially if you are a heavy sweater during races). Many people will avoid high fiber foods like cereals, salads, and certain fruits a day or two before a race, as they can create gastrointestinal issues during a race for some people.

On the morning of a race, it is a good idea to eat your pre-race meal at least 3 hours before the race begins. This should allow you to digest most of it before the start, preventing it from sloshing around your stomach (or worse), while allowing you to eat whatever you normally eat, since it has time to digest. If you are close to three hours, this pre-race meal should be mainly carbs, with a little bit of protein thrown in – and should not be large. One of us has done well limiting this three-hour-before meal, even when doing a half ironman, to a PowerBar and a bagel, with some Gatorade to wash it down. We know others who swear by English Muffins and peanut butter or by yogurt and a banana. Coffee can be great to get your body awakened and fuel your race, but know how your body responds to caffeine. If you are not used to drinking it, caffeine can cause GI distress. Consuming some electrolytes like sodium, potassium, and magnesium, perhaps in pills or capsules, or dissolved in a drink (using a Nuun or FIZZ tablet), can have benefits in helping you absorb fluids better and possibly avoid some muscle cramping. A last-minute GU with a small dose of carbs and caffeine has also served us well. Of course, we know there are other theories and practices, and we will cover how to obtain nutrition during the race in later chapters.

Tip Eleven: Learn what works for you nutritionally and, just as importantly, what doesn't.

Dealing with Bathroom Needs

When You've Got to Go, You've Got to Go

The Escape from Alcatraz triathlon is one of the best races in the world. Besides the incredible history, it also has many unique aspects such as sand ladders, steps, deep sand, hills, single track, no swim buoys, strong current, cold water, . . . and a boat ride that takes you out to Alcatraz before you jump off to start the race.

The logistics of race morning require some planning and a good deal of time to get everything done prior to the race start. You have to park near the first transition, catch a bus that takes you to the ferry terminal, and then take the boat to Alcatraz Island. Once you board the boat, you're on it for about a half hour or so depending on how early you boarded. There is a bathroom on board, but as you can imagine, almost EVERYONE has nervous pre-race energy and the line is too long, with the thousands of anxious athletes all having needs. So, by now, you can probably imagine where this is going.

The water in the bay is cold, typically in the low to mid 50 degree Fahrenheit range, so all of the competitors wear wetsuits for the swim. On the ride out to Alcatraz, the mass of people struggle into their wetsuits and start to line up or edge toward the doors for the brave jump into the chilly waters. Most triathletes know that a lot of people will pee in their wetsuits prior to the start of a race, usually because they have to go again but also sometimes for warmth. I know, it sounds disgusting if you're just hearing about it for the first time. Who am I kidding, yes, it's disgusting no matter how you look at it. But, usually, this is done in the water prior to the start. As I mentioned, though, for Alcatraz you jump off the boat and have to start swimming right away.

Okay, so prior to this race you can literally look around and see the 'flow' coming from the legs of people's wetsuits as you're getting ready to start. Oh, and one thing that I failed to mention is that the floor inside the boat is carpeted. I don't know how they clean it afterwards, but it must be really nasty!

Originally, I thought that maybe it wasn't as bad as I was imagining; maybe I was just around a group of people who had no problem urinating on carpet, with weak bladders, or just drank too much. But, my suspicions were confirmed when Andy Potts, who had won the race, mentioned seeing many people peeing on the boat during his victory speech. So, if you ever get the privilege of participating in this great race, you're forewarned. D.W.

While it is not the most pleasant thing to talk about, eliminating your waste products before the start of a race is a big deal! Once a race begins and the clock is ticking, you don't want to spend time in a porta-potty or in the woods taking care of business. And you don't want to be constantly fighting the urge to go as you race. Moreover, some of us have an aversion to peeing in our uniforms or wetsuits right before the race starts or during a race.

As suggested above, being careful about when and what you eat and drink can help to manage this issue. Again, pay attention to what works and what doesn't. We wish we could give you a definitive list, but everyone is different. Just between the two of us, our lists are vastly different. But it also pays to have a peeing and pooping plan for each race. Your plan should be influenced by how close the race venue is to your home or hotel, what the bathroom and porta-potty facilities are like at the race venue, what you are going to be wearing at the race, and your own metabolism.

If you're lucky and/or wealthy enough, your hotel or home may be right near the start line and you can go at the last minute in a private bathroom. However, that is a rare occurrence and most frequently you will have to use the race porta-potties, which are typically disgusting, hot, smelly, and often do not have enough toilet paper. It sounds funny, but if you can, scout out in advance which porta-potties you want to use, study the start times of the

different waves, and then estimate where and when the lines are likely to be shorter. There are often random ones set off a bit that people don't notice with shorter lines. However, account for the possibility that the crowds may be bigger than expected, or that you may have to use the facilities more than once. Bring extra toilet paper or tissues with you, as well as wet-wipes. They may come in handy if they run out of toilet paper or if you have to duck into the woods to relieve yourself because the lines are too long. Trust us, toilet paper is often the most prized and sought after race-day equipment! If you are wearing a wetsuit in the race, don't put it on until the last minute so that you won't have to remove it again to answer a final call of nature.

Tip Twelve: Expect to have to use the porta-john and for there to be a line, so have a plan.

**Bonus Tip: Bringing your own toilet paper can save you a lot of grief!

Preparing Gear and Equipment

Sabotage

At large races, including World and National Championships, they usually require you to rack your bike in the transition area the day before the race. This can complicate travel plans and it can also require additional planning around things like how much to fill your tires with air (not so high so that you risk a tube bursting if the bike is sitting in the hot sun), how/whether to cover your bike overnight if rain is a possibility, and how to prevent sabotage on your bike. Yes – sabotage! I know of at least two cases where friends of mine, who were threats to win their age groups, were apparent victims of unsportsmanlike overnight shenanigans. In Lausanne, Switzerland at the Age-Group World Championships in 2006, one of our friends claims that someone had loosened her handlebar bolt, making it impossible for her to hold her aerobars up. And at the Age-Group World Championships in London in 2013, another friend says someone messed up his gearing, making it impossible for him to go into his large chain ring. Both athletes had ridden their bikes the day before and examined them religiously before racking them. However, they both failed to give their bikes a careful once-over on race morning and the results were disappointing – although, fortunately, no one got hurt. P.B.

Tip Thirteen: Perform a thorough race-morning equipment check.

A careful check of all your gear and equipment at the last minute can prevent much disappointment. Make sure your bike steers appropriately, that its gears are shifting properly and are set for where you want them to begin the race (e.g., in easiest gear if the bike course starts with an uphill), that the brakes and cyclometer are not rubbing (and are working), and that the pedals are screwed on (see the second story at the start of this chapter). One of the most common issues when traveling and having to put your bike back together is having aerobars drop on you. This has happened to us more than once, even after checking for it carefully, and it was very frustrating. If possible, having bike support check your bike over (typically for free) can save you quite a few headaches.

You also want to be sure that your tires are filled appropriately for the conditions. If the roads are rough, filling the tires much over 120 psi will risk a blowout or flat. And when it's wet or raining, keeping tire pressure lower can give you better traction on turns. Indeed, for safety and stability, one of us now races at 95 psi using wider, 25mm tires. On top of that, make sure your bike shoes, socks (if you are wearing them – we recommend them for longer races), helmet, sunglasses, headbands, running shoes, race belt, and nutrition products are all lined up in a way that others will not kick them or grab them. Still, not every calamity can be prevented by last minute checking, especially if you don't do it carefully enough.

Calamity Jane

As you can tell by now, my wife, Shelly, is a Calamity Jane. At one Age-Group Duathlon National Championship race in Tucson,

Arizona, she had her rear wheel dislodge from the seat stays as she was doing a U-turn half way through the bike leg. This time it was her fault, as she had not shoved the wheel on far enough when reassembling her bike. Fortunately, she did not take a tumble and was able to quickly dismount and shove the wheel back on, only losing a minute or so in the process. In another Age-Group World Championship triathlon race in Auckland, New Zealand, she goofed up again. This time she failed to tighten her aerobars enough during reassembly, leading them to constantly move up and down with every bump, keeping her from staying in a truly aero position. Finally, in an Age-Group National Championship race out in California (for Aquathlon – run, swim, run), her brand new, but overly tight, Team USA tri-suit split up the back while she was warming up. Luckily, her sister came to the rescue with a set of safety pins two minutes before the start, allowing her to compete without revealing too much to everyone. P.B.

Warming Up Your Body and Final Prep

Frigid Water

The water temperature in Lake Geneva was in the low 60s for the Age-Group World Championships in Lausanne, Switzerland and, up until that time, I had not swum in water that cold. The Olympic Distance Triathlon race for which I had qualified was scheduled for a Saturday, but they also allowed anyone who qualified for that race to enter the Aquathlon race on Thursday (in this case, they made it a swim-run, since run-swim-run would not work if you had to put on and remove a wetsuit). Since my wife loves Aquathlon and was going to do it, I decided I would take a crack at it too. Thinking I could handle the cold water with a wetsuit on and not taking the race that seriously, I didn't do any warm-up before the start and just dove right in off the starting dock when the horn went off.

As soon as I hit that cold water, it took my breath away and I started to hyperventilate. I had never experienced a feeling like that and it really scared me, and it was all I could do to swim over to a kayak that was monitoring the course about 50 meters away.

The kayaker asked me if I wanted to be taken back to shore and I said "Yes, after I catch my breath a bit." But after a minute or two, my heart rate slowed down and I felt somewhat acclimated to the cold water, and I told the kayaker that she should keep an eye on me while I tried to complete the 1000 meter swim. Well, I finished the swim (slowly), took about 5 minutes to struggle out of my wetsuit with my frozen fingers, and then ran pretty fast on the 5K run -- which still didn't allow me to avoid finishing dead last in the whole race!

This humbling experience taught me several lessons. First, I never try to swim in a cold-water race without first doing a practice swim to re-familiarize myself with the feelings that icy water creates. I usually try to do this a day before a race, not counting on there being a place to do a warm-up swim the morning of the race (since in big races, warm-ups are often not possible). I also learned that it's helpful to do some dynamic warm-ups in my wetsuit before starting – some simple arm and leg swings, as well as knee lifts and calf stretches. If I can get in the water before, I won't swim very far, but I will do some quick, hard strokes. At the very least, I will dunk my head in the water, let the chill hit my face, and make sure my goggles are on properly. This approach worked for me in the triathlon race in Lausanne, two days after the last-place Aquathlon experience, and it has continued to work for me in about a half dozen races that I have done since then that have had water temps in the high-50s. P.B.

Tip Fourteen: Doing a warm up to get your blood pumping before a race can make a huge difference, especially in colder races.

It's good to do some spinning if possible or running with a couple of short pick-ups to get the heart rate up so that you avoid the lag that can happen if you start a race cold. But, whether you can bike and run or not, the most important thing to do before a race is to swim a bit, if at all possible. This helps get the heart rate up, warms up your shoulder muscles so they don't get really tight when you take it out harder than you meant to, which inevitably happens, acclimates you to the water, and it has been suggested that this would help avoid many of the swimming deaths that occur. You want to do this close to the start of the race. It's always amusing to see people an hour and a half prior to an event putting in a serious warm-up. While that's better than nothing, it's basically just getting rid of nervous energy at that point.

As important as it is to get used to the water, it's just as important to familiarize yourself with the transition area before the race begins. Do a practice jog from the swim-out to your transition spot, go jog out to where the mount and dismount lines are for the bike course (and do a practice mounting and dismounting if they let you bring your bike out there – which often they won't), do another practice jog from the bike-in gate to your transition spot, and finally do a practice jog through the run-out gate. Notice where things seem crowded or where the ground is muddy, slippery, rocky, or bumpy. This may influence what you decide to do about when to put on and take off your bike shoes. We will talk more about this in the T1 and T2 chapters. Check your bike and transition set-up one last time and then go off to the swim start.

Tip Fifteen: Know the ins-and-outs of the transition area -- literally!

It is important to try to say calm and relaxed throughout all these last minute preparations. This is sometimes very hard to do with the pre-race music blaring over loudspeakers, the race announcer warning you about all kinds of things, or friends complaining to you about one of their difficulties. Some dynamic warm-ups and stretches can help calm you down, as can visualizing what you will do after the race. Think about the meal or the entertainment you plan to experience when you're done, or find someone to talk about something other than triathlon!

Applying the PREPARE Approach

It should be fairly apparent how the words in the **PREPARE** acronym apply to pre-race travel and set-up. To begin, we can't stress enough the importance of having a **Plan** for everything that you want to happen before the race starts. You need packing plans (or checklists), travel plans, sleeping and rest plans, nutrition plans, peeing and pooping plans, gear and transition area plans, and warm-up plans. And you need contingency plans or Plan Bs of ways to do things if the original ones are sidetracked.

It helps to **Rehearse** how you will execute these plans; some practice sessions on setting up transitions or doing warm-ups can help, even for the most experienced athletes. Of course, some of this rehearsal comes through experience over time, as you pack more, travel more, and race more, learning the ropes and the do's and don'ts. But, no matter what, don't plan to try anything brand new in a race – unless you are a total novice at racing.

Being religious about how you **Execute** the different plans should pay dividends, but since surprises can arise, you want to be mentally flexible enough to switch to a contingency plan or Plan B if necessary. For example, when you get to the race venue and they won't let you do a practice swim or take your bike out for a test mount and dismount, have some other warm-up techniques ready to go.

Learning to **Persist** may not seem especially relevant to pre-race travel and set-up, except if you are dealing with traffic jams, long lines at packet pick-up and porta-potties, or complicated set-up procedures (such as what can happen at point-to-point races where you have two different transition areas). It is very important not to lose your cool or become stressed out by these occurrences. For instance, if someone cuts in line at the porta-potties, don't bawl them out in front of everyone. You don't want to use up emotional and physical energy that could be devoted to racing.

If something goes wrong during pre-race travel and set-up, spend time after the race and **Analyze** what caused it. It probably won't be too hard to figure out what caused a travel delay or the forgetting of an important piece of equipment. It may be harder to figure out why someone would deliberately sabotage your bike or why a meal that you have eaten many times before caused pre-race stomach distress on this occasion.

When you think you have figured what worked and what didn't, **Revise** your various plans for future races. Avoid an airline that seems to lose your baggage too often or have too many delays. Stay away from certain roads. Pack extra clothing to account for varying weather conditions.

Finally, as we said at the outset, **Enjoy** what you are doing! Don't let pre-race problems sour you on the sport. While this part of racing can be stressful, there are other portions of the racing experience, discussed in later chapters, that will probably test your emotions even more.

3 – SWIMMING

Whether you're a novice or an All-American swimmer, the swim at the start of a triathlon can be daunting. You've heard the horror stories, we're sure; kicks to the head or chest, people pulling on your feet, being boxed in and not being able to move, getting dunked, swallowing a gulp of water, not being able to see, getting sea sick, and on and on. A lot can happen on the swim, although those occurrences are relatively rare. But they can and do sometimes happen, so it's best to be prepared for them mentally. And, don't be intimidated if you have or develop a fear for the swims. It is more common than you would imagine and we've even seen some of the top professionals start to succumb to pre-swim panic attacks subsequent to a rough event. However, with time and practice you can overcome your fears and maybe even learn to enjoy the swim. By learning how to deal with different situations, you can out-swim many stronger swimmers by outsmarting them! We've used that to our advantage at many races, but we've also had to learn the hard way about different unexpected circumstances ourselves.

Opening the Floodgates

Racing in the Age-Group Olympic-Distance National Championships in Tuscaloosa, Alabama in the middle of August, 2009 did not seem like the greatest idea. It was likely to be beastly hot and humid, and not a place where we could perform our best.

But for a chance to qualify for the Age-Group World Championships in Gold Coast, Australia the following Spring (Fall in Australia), we decided to make the trip. It rained like cats and dogs during our long drive down there from North Carolina, but we welcomed that since we thought it would cool things down. Indeed, the next day, we scouted out the course and even did a short practice swim in the very calm Black Warrior River, and we thought the race conditions were going to be much better than we originally feared. Boy – were we wrong!

The rainstorm, which was a remnant of a tropical storm, had caused the river to start to flood upstream from the race venue, so without telling the race participants that they were doing so, the water management folks opened the locks on the river and allowed all the water to flow downstream, just before the race started. This turned a calm river into one with a strong (and filthy) current, and I, along with numerous others, didn't handle it very well.

I was in the first swim wave and we were supposed to keep a hand on the dock until the gun went off. I knew something was amiss when I could hardly hold on to the dock as the water tried to pull me away. But since the first 200 meters of the swim were with the current, I just streamlined my body as I took off and tried to take advantage of the extra boost. That worked fine until I spotted the first turn buoy that required me to make a right hand turn and then swim across the current about 100 meters to another right-hand turn buoy. After making that first right turn, I realized that I was being pulled further and further away from the next buoy, no matter how hard I swam. With an exhausting effort, I finally made it to the buoy and then started the arduous process of swimming the 1,200 meters I needed to go against the current before I could turn toward the swim exit – the swim start and swim exit were widely separated in this race, leading to 6 times the amount of upstream swimming as downstream swimming. This long stretch took forever. I can remember looking at a high rise dormitory on the river bank and wondering why I couldn't pass it.

Eventually, I got to the last upstream buoy, had an awful time getting around it to make a right turn, and then managed to swim across the current about 100 meters to get to the swim exit. As I looked at my watch, it read well over an hour – at least twice the amount of time I had hoped for – and I knew my qualification for Australia was doomed.

My wife, Shelly, handled it much better as she went off 5 minutes after me. She watched what happened to me after the first buoy and drew on her background as a sailing instructor (during college summers) to determine that she needed to overcompensate a ton and aim way, way right as she swam across the current to the second right-turn buoy. And then she realized that it would be advantageous to do two other things on the upstream leg. Draft a really big guy (she's pretty small herself) and stay away from all the debris and muck that seemed to be thickest near the shore. While her swim turned out about 15 minutes longer than usual, it made her very competitive in her age group and she eventually finished fourth and qualified for Australia.

After the race, I went to the Slowtwitch.com forum (for triathlon discussions) to see what people were saying about the swim. One engineering type had it all figured out, and I have to admit that his explanation made me feel better, since his numbers coincided perfectly with what we and other friends – including my co-author, Coach Dave – had experienced:

"I just ran a quick model for an out and back course assuming that current speed translated directly into changes in relative speed (i.e., a 1 mph current would make the swimmer 1 mph faster relative to the shore when going downstream and 1 mph slower relative to the shore when going upstream. The following are the results:

·   *A 21 minute 1500m swimmer would be expected to take about 28 minutes if the current speed was a uniform 1.35 mph.*

·   *A person who is a 25 minute 1500m swimmer would take about 39 minutes if the current speed was a uniform 1.35 mph, or a 14-minute penalty*

· *A person who is a 30 minute 1500m swimmer would take about 62 minutes if the current speed was a uniform 1.35 mph, or a 32-minute penalty."*

Nationals were in Tuscaloosa again the following year and I lobbied to skip it. The memories of not being able to get past that dormitory were just too vivid. I won that debate and we ended up competing in more local races that year. P.B.

Tip One: Pay attention to what's happening in earlier waves, if possible, and remember that everyone is struggling with the same conditions.

We realize this can be very difficult at times, but it's best to save your energy and stay calm. People can do all sorts of crazy things on the course that will drive you crazy. Some will be obviously intentional, while others are just due to inexperience or poor decisions. Whatever the case, roll with it and move on with your own race as best you can.

The Blockade Swimmer

Pool swim triathlons can be a lot of fun with a time trial start and often a less crowded course, since large groups aren't all starting at once. Being a former collegiate swimmer, I'm typically one of the faster swimmers in the triathlons that I enter. Going into an early-season pool swim triathlon, my main competition was a friend that I had had numerous very close races with. I was a better swimmer than he was, we were very similar on the bike, and he was typically a little better on the run.

Well, my 'friend' figured out a way to take away my advantage. Typically, these races start everyone 10 seconds apart and have the swimmers zig-zag through the lanes. Competitors sent in their 100-yard pace before the race and the start list is seeded accordingly, with the fastest swimmer going first, the second fastest going second, and so on. Can you catch on to the diabolical strategy?

Yep, my rival put in a pace that he knew would be faster than anything that I would put in so that he would start the race 10-seconds ahead of me. I didn't catch on to his full plan until after the race started and I quickly caught up to him. Knowing that he couldn't lose any more than 10-seconds to me, he purposely swam slowly and wouldn't let me pass throughout the swim! Thus, not only did he take away my normal gains on the swim, he also got to relax and not waste any energy like he usually did in the water.

Frustrating for sure! But, I was powerless to do anything about it. I've got to give him credit for being clever, but that does rank up there as pretty bad unsportsmanlike conduct. D.W.

Tip Two: Don't let other competitors get under your skin.

A disaster during the swim can be unbelievably discouraging. It can exhaust you and leave you cramped and gasping, and it can make you overly anxious before the swim start of your next race. We have shared stories already about problems during the swim that can arise from mistakes in packing (forgotten goggles, overly tight suits), planning (for porta-potty lines), or warm-ups (testing ice cold water). And, our opening stories for this chapter point to how swim problems can arise because of unexpected weather events or bad behavior from competitors. It is hard to plan or rehearse for these kinds of problems, although practicing swimming in rough water, as well as getting comfortable breathing on either side, can pay dividends when high winds or tides create choppy water that makes sighting buoys difficult.

Tip Three: Practice open water techniques prior to race day. The same can even go for practicing the turns and passing people during pool swim triathlons.

Don't be a fish out of water during a race! You can practice dealing with many potential obstacles that you will face in the open water with pool drills. Some of these include swimming with your eyes closed, drafting behind friends, swimming three or four abreast in a lane, having partners all starting at the same time as you, sighting on various things on the deck while swimming, and having people purposely splashing you and making waves while you swim. For pool swims, doing repeats where you perform quick turns while switching lanes under the lane rope and practice passing slower swimmers in tight spaces will have you showing up to the event much more confident than scared.

Other problems can arise because of:

- Complicated, crowded, or confusing starts

- Difficult-to-follow courses

- Cramping

- Challenging swim exits

Here are some entertaining stories and tips about what we've learned under each of these headings. We discuss how the PREPARE approach can help with the swim leg at the end of the chapter.

Complicated, Crowded, or Confusing Starts

Watch Out for Photographers

Another potty story! This one is about an age-group national championships race many years ago. They had us line up well in advance of our wave start in corrals to keep everything running smoothly. So, I got in the first corral and started getting ready. I realized that I started to feel the need to have to relieve myself again, thanks to those ever-present nerves on race morning. But, I thought at this point that I could manage to get into the race and I'd be fine. Fast forward a bit and now we've moved up to the last corral and I stood on the beach waiting to get into the water. By now, my eyes were watering and I just couldn't hold it any more. So, I let go as we were standing on the beach. I tried my hardest to be discreet because I didn't want to draw any attention to myself, plus I thought it was pretty disgusting. Of course, I would find out later that it's very common! So, I was looking down at the sand by my feet, which was obviously becoming wet and the front of my suit was much more discolored than I had expected. Shoot! I kept moving my feet and tried to hide behind people, but being a good swimmer I wanted to make sure that I started in the front of the pack. Just then, I finally looked up. What?! Of course, there was a race videographer with his video camera standing directly in front of us with his camera pointed at me! Any press is good press, right? I'm not so sure about that. I never saw the coverage or post-race video for that race so I don't know if I made the cut, but perhaps I don't want to know... D.W.

Head-on Crash in a Lake

My first attempt to do a triathlon was in a moderately large sprint race in North Carolina that had a half-mile swim in a small lake, a 15 mile bike, and a 5K run. I had competed in this race the year before as part of a team, doing the run portion, and I thought I could handle the whole thing. But as I racked my clunky mountain bike in transition alongside all the racing and triathlon bikes, I thought I might be biting off more than I could chew. That turned out to be the case.

The opening moments of the swim are what did me in, not the clunky bike. To begin with, I was freaked out by the 100 or so aggressive swimmers that all churned into the water at the same time. I tried to let them go way ahead of me, but then I had no one to follow, and I quickly became disoriented in the water and didn't know which direction to swim. Unfortunately, I picked the wrong direction to my left and I was actually swimming out into the group of swimmers coming into the swim finish. Thus, I crashed head on into a few of the faster swimmers from an earlier swim-start wave, and I had to endure a nasty string of epithets from several of them. Seeing what a ruckus I was creating, I decided to quit the race and save myself from further abuse and embarrassment.

Still, a year later, I came back to try again. This time I started swimming in the right direction, but almost immediately, with all of the thrashing about, I had the one and only panic attack that I have ever had in my life, which sent my heartbeat racing. I decided to quit this race too, although this time, after sneaking out of the swim area, I did a practice ride of the bike course, as well as a practice run, and jumped off the course right before the finish line so that I wouldn't be counted as a finisher.

Determined to make the third time a charm, I entered the race again the next year. I had purchased a new road bike, which made me a little more confident. Also, I had been practicing swimming more than in previous years. I started the swim way out to the side, so I could be in calmer water and also keep an eye on where the other swimmers were going, which worked well. Although I swam very slowly, I didn't go off course, didn't bump into anyone, and didn't panic. I ended up finishing the whole race as one of the last competitors, but I was exhilarated and, frankly, hooked for life! I'm still at the sport and still improving, twenty years later! P.B.

The swim start of a triathlon can be unbelievably chaotic and confusing. This especially applies to open-water swims that usually have many people starting at once. All kinds of things can happen to throw you off your game. One must determine: where and how to warm up, what lines you are supposed to wait in, where to relieve yourself at the last minute, where to line up in the water in relation to the other swimmers, where to wet and secure your goggles, and where to store things that you don't want to leave in transition but don't want to give up until right before you start (e.g., flip flops to protect your feet from a rocky beach, a jacket to keep you warm while waiting – some races have bag drop-offs for this). We have already reported some of our problems with warming up, final peeing and pooping, and lining up. And we can assure you that we have experienced other problems including having leaky, non-functional goggles, getting goggles kicked off, being punched in the ribs and head as everyone takes off, and cutting our hands and feet on docks, rocks, and the fingernails of other competitors.

The issues highlighted above should not be left for spur-of-the-moment decisions. Scout out the swim start as best you can before the race. Know where bag drop-offs (if any) will be, where

the porta-potties will be, where the corrals will be and how early you have to line up, where sharp objects might be, and where you want to line up versus the other swimmers.

Your call on where to line up should be influenced by a whole range of factors, including how strong a swimmer you are, which side you favor when breathing, which way the waves and current are pulling, where the sun is, and how easy it is to sight the first buoy. If you are a weaker swimmer and you tend to breathe to your right, it might make sense to start on the left side, so that you will see other swimmers on each breath and can use them for directional guidance. This is especially the case if the first buoy is one that you must go around on the right and the distance from the start to that buoy is shortest from the left side of the start. But if starting from the left and breathing to your right will have you constantly staring into the sun or facing into crashing waves, be willing to start in a different spot or breathe in a different direction. It helps to watch the swimmers that go off in earlier waves to see the difficulties they are encountering or, better yet, what strategies they are using to deal with current, sun, waves, and buoy placement.

Tip Four: Know the specifics of the race to allow ample time race-morning for swim bags and corrals, as well as, figuring out the best swimming strategies.

Introduction to Open Water Swimming

My first open water race was quite a memorable experience. I was down in Florida with my team for the swimming national championships when I was a senior in high school. As it turns out, the 5k open water national championships just so happened to be that same weekend after we were done with our events. So, my coach signed us up for it. Being a distance swimmer, I loved the thought of it and the challenge of racing that far. Forget that I had never swum in open water like that before, let alone in the ocean, I was young and invincible!

Then, as luck would have it, the water was very choppy race morning due to a storm a little ways away. The race organizers made an announcement that it was 'swim at your own risk' – we were warned, but the race would go on. We started a couple hundred yards off of the beach, but had to swim parallel to the surf for about 500 yards before turning away from it. Being inexperienced in the current and the chop, I kept getting pushed in toward the surf and bumped several times into the person on the inside of me. I guess it got to be too much, because suddenly the person grabs me around the neck and lifts me up long enough for me to see that it was a female with a University of Florida swim cap on and for her to proceed to punch me in the face! Another lesson quickly learned was that Swedish goggles, which I wore in pool races, were not great for open water, especially when getting punched. I had a nice ring around my eye from that one.

Embarrassed, but with more desire than ever to race hard, I put my head down and hammered away. After maybe twenty minutes and after making a couple of turns, I felt like I was swimming really fast and didn't see anyone in front of me. Wow, was I winning? Nope, once again my ego was deflated when a kayaker stopped me to inform me that I had swum way off course. UGH.

Course correction made, I got back on track, but the waves were relentless and I proceeded to get extremely seasick! I started throwing up in the water, trying to not let the swimmers behind me swim through it. I'd swim for a few minutes with my head spinning before having to stop and puke again. It was a long time before that sea sick feeling faded away, long after the race was over. As unlikely as it may seem, I did finish and would go on to become a pretty decent open water swimmer. But, my start was anything but stellar! D.W.

Another factor to consider is whether it is a beach start, where everyone in your start wave runs into the water together, or an in-water start – which can involve taking off from a dock or pier, usually with your hand touching it rather than diving from it, or from floating on your own with everyone else. With an in-water start, as you might imagine from our earlier stories, many people will use this as an opportunity to pee a final time. Indeed, in cold water, many people swear by this final pee as a way to warm up their wetsuits.

As you wait for the gun (or horn) to go off, put your watch in stopwatch mode and take several deep breaths, doing everything you can to keep yourself relaxed and calm. Have you ever watched the start of a race and found it comical to watch people hitting their watches instead of taking off right away. However brief, this can cause you to lose the second or two it would take to get beside or ahead of someone or miss out on an important draft. We recommend starting the watch a bit earlier than the actual start. Those ten or fifteen seconds aren't going to mess up your data that much and will leave you focused on the actual start of the race. If it is a beach start, when the gun goes off you want to run into the water with your legs kicking sideways above the water for as long as you can to try to limit resistance from the water. You should run as far as possible before diving in as long as you can lift your feet over the surface, since you can usually run in shallow water lower than knee level faster than you can swim. Then, if the water is still shallow enough, do a few dolphin dives to quickly get you out into deeper open water ahead of your competition.

Tip Five: Start your watch a little bit before the gun is about to go off so that you can focus on the start of the race instead of your wrist.

Once in the water from a run, or from an in-water start, you want to get into a relaxed, steady rhythm as soon as possible. If you start out too hard, especially if you haven't warmed up adequately, your lats and shoulders will burn and tire quickly. Then, you're stuck having to slow down and/or swim uncomfortably. Take it out fast, but under control and relatively comfortable. Back off before you get to the burning fatigue if you feel it coming on. Breathing every other stroke at first can help you relax, as it can keep you from feeling winded and help you establish a rhythm. Keep your wits about you and don't let people slapping, hitting, or scratching you throw you off. Expect this to happen and be surprised if it doesn't. You don't need a lot of space to swim well and if people are crowding you, just try to rotate a bit more, keep your recovery a bit closer to your body, or do other small adjustments that won't slow you down.

If you are a really good swimmer and/or have practiced it a lot, it may make sense to go a little harder at the start to get some separation from the other swimmers or to allow you to find a group of faster swimmers who you might draft. Otherwise, just staying relaxed and steady is the key.

Tip Six: Stay under control at the start of the swim. You shouldn't feel your shoulders or lats burning right away.

Foreign Language

I had rough swim starts to two different Ironman races. Not necessarily because of the crowded start or people pushing and shoving, but because I got surprised by the gun going off! At Ironman Austria they had monitors holding up a rope at the edge of the beach to keep people from going in the water. Then, maybe a hundred yards out in the water there was another marked area. The idea, as I understood it, was that they would let the swimmers in shortly before the start to get up to the start line and then the official gun would sound. However, as it got closer and closer to 7am, I started to wonder why they weren't letting us in yet. When they finally did let us go, I started to somewhat casually swim out to where I thought we were supposed to wait again only to realize that people had already taken off! I still don't know if I didn't hear the gun because I thought I had more time or what. But, that was the first time where I got stuck in the middle of a pack of people and had no ability to move away due to the sheer size of the pack. I was capable of moving much faster but had no choice but to swim easy for at least half of the swim with the group until I could break free a bit.

The second occurrence was at Ironman Brazil. I don't like to swim with my watch, so I took it off and went to line up on the beach 15-20 minutes before the start so that I could get on the front line.

What I didn't expect, but shouldn't have been surprised by, was that all of the pre-race announcements were in Portuguese. So, I had no idea what was being said. At one point, the announcer started to get excited and I thought we were getting ready to go, but then I almost had a false start when everyone just let out a big cheer! I don't know what was said, but it was something fun to get everyone pumped up, obviously. So, I relaxed and tried to focus on the people around me. Of course, right when my attention wavered, the gun goes off and I was taken by surprise again. UGH! I had to do some maneuvering around people that had jumped in front of me and got kicked a bit. It was nothing too bad, but should have been avoidable! D.W.

Difficult-to-Follow Courses

Lost in the Pool

In one pool-swim triathlon, my wife and I seeded ourselves with the same estimated time, so the race director started me 10 seconds ahead of her in a time-trial format. For this race, we swam down one lane, turned left under the lane divider, swam back down the next lane, turned right under the next lane divider, and so on, until we swam 500 yards (it was a big pool!).

Everything was going fine for the first 250 yards. I could see Shelly behind me as I made each turn. But as I made the left turn at 275 yards, Shelly inexplicably turned right and she didn't hear me yell at her that she turned the wrong way. Yes – a less competitive husband would have gone after her before she went too far, but I didn't want to mess up my race, too, and I thought she would figure it out soon enough. Well, it took her four lengths going in the wrong direction before someone grabbed her and set her straight. And while the rule would have allowed her to jump out of the pool and re-enter the pool where she made the wrong turn, she re-swam the 4 additional lengths, adding 100 yards to the 500 yard swim.

During the award ceremony, as he was handing Shelly her first-place age-group prize (which she won by three seconds), the race director said that this was the first time in all his years managing triathlons that he had seen someone get lost in a pool swim. P.B.

Lead or Follow?

I'm always amazed at how people would rather follow swimmers zigzagging through the water, or even go way off course, rather than risk losing their feet while trying to sight for themselves. I could actually write countless stories about this phenomenon that I have seen through the years, from ITU (International Triathlon Union) pro waves swimming to the wrong buoys, pros missing a buoy, people swimming perpendicular to the actual course, etc., but there is one that really stands out for me.

I did an Ironman back in the day when Phil Liggett, of Tour de France commentating fame, announced the race for TV coverage. It's always fun to listen to Phil's expert commentary and off-the-cuff remarks. At this race, the professionals started at the same time as the rest of the competitors, just with a bit of a lead. The race was a two-loop course in the ocean with a standard rectangular route. I got out to a pretty good start and found myself near the front of a pack and behind a group of pros in front of us.

I'm typically very good at swimming a straight line and sighting in open water races and have used that to gain time on competitors numerous times. So, as I came up to the second turn buoy I was surprised to see that a couple of the swimmers in the front pack had cut the turn too hard and were swimming toward the wrong buoy! I was even more surprised when the people ahead and with me in my pack started to follow them!! Having done my own sighting and scouting the course, I ditched the group and swam quickly in the correct direction toward the beach.

The video coverage was hilarious, as you could see 1500 people starting to swim in the wrong direction. But even better, Phil Liggett mentioned me several times because I was in fourth place on the swim out of the first loop and still up toward the front after the whole swim - as a young age-grouper! They even showed me getting out of the water. I still consider this my very brief claim to fame; that Phil Liggett said my name on TV.

It doesn't matter how fast of a swimmer you are. If you don't swim in a straight line, then you're giving up time to someone who does! D.W.

Tip Seven: Count how many buoys are in the water and know which way you'll be turning. Don't trust everyone else to know what they're doing!

We have seen or gone off course ourselves in open-water swims more times than we care to remember. The causes have been numerous and sometimes humorous. At the Age-Group World Championships in Auckland, New Zealand in 2012, rough water with high waves (and 58 degree temperature) made it hard for both of us, as well as other competing friends, to spot buoys and see where we were going. We probably both swam an extra quarter mile and had much longer swim times than we hoped for, plus staying in the frigid water for that extra time made it harder for us to transition and get going on the bike. And bright sun behind a turn buoy at the Age-Group National Championships in Burlington, Vermont in 2012 caused us not to see that buoy and just follow others who were also going off course. Fortunately, only a few of our competitors got it right and our finishing places were probably not affected very much. In other races, fogged-up goggles have been a problem and have led to heading for the wrong buoys. And taking a longer, less-direct route around guide buoys when the rules allow you to go on either side of guide buoys has lead to swimming extra distances. It pays to listen at pre-race meetings when the rules are described.

Staying on course can be assisted by having goggles that fit right, don't fog or leak, and that darken the sun. To reiterate, it also helps to scout out the swim course really well before you start. You should know the number of buoys before each turn, the rules about passing those buoys, and some on-shore buildings, trees, or towers that you can sight behind turn buoys or swim exits in case rough water makes it hard to see.

Tip Eight: In most races, the only buoys that you have to be on a certain side are the turn buoys. The others are sight or guide buoys that you can be on either side of.

Practicing your sighting while you swim prior to racing is essential and, in difficult situations, you should be prepared to sight often, perhaps on every third or fourth stroke. Too many people think that sighting slows them down, so they wait too long before trying to see where they are going. Invariably, these same people have to make many at least slight adjustments and/or throw their strokes off by having to look around for the buoy. If you sight often, it's okay if you don't see your buoy or swim exit once or twice, you can still stick to your efficient stroke and swim straight. However, if you don't sight often you'll have to make those corrections each time and keep your head up higher or longer to make sure you see what you're looking for.

Even if you're not a triathlete yourself, you've probably heard stories of people getting kicked, hit, dunked, and pulled on during the swim. Many people seem to actually do this on purpose trying to keep closest to the turn buoys or stay with a certain person. If you watch a race on television, you'll see how much time these people lose compared to those that are smart enough to perhaps swim a little extra, but in clean water.

Tip Nine: Sight often and don't purposely swim on top of other people, even around turn buoys.

Clean Water

At the Olympic distance world championships in Honolulu, there was a large crowd gathered right in the middle of the starting area. I had learned through experience, that the swim is even tougher at the higher-level races because the quality of the field is both faster and less spread out. So, I decided to go out to the far outside right before the gun went off. I got a clean start and kept fresh water in front of me as I could literally see the other fast group all fighting with each other. It was such a big difference that I came out of the water first in my wave that year by about a full 20 seconds. And, it wasn't because I was a faster swimmer. No, there were several who could have easily swum faster than I could. But, I had chosen a cleaner path. D.W.

As suggested earlier, practicing how to breathe on either side can pay dividends if bright sun or waves make it desirable to breathe in one direction over another. If you feel like you're going off course, don't hesitate to pause your freestyle and do a breast stroke for a few seconds to get your bearings. And by all means, if you see someone doing just breaststroke at a speed as fast as your freestyle, draft that person, since he/she is able to see exactly where he/she is going.

Cramping

Seizing at the Start

On our way from our home in North Carolina to a summer vacation in Martha's Vineyard a few years back, we decided to stop off overnight in northeast Maryland to do an Olympic Distance race called Diamond in the Rough. Well, the race turned out to be rough alright! Shelly and I were assigned to the same starting wave in the open-water (Susquehanna River) swim, so we planned to try to swim together, and I was hoping to draft off her. For the start, we had to swim out to a deep-water area between two buoys and tread water for 3 minutes. But while we were waiting for the gun to go off, I lost her. I looked around for her frantically, but then the starting horn went off and I decided that I better take off, abandoning our drafting plan. I didn't see Shelly again until I approached the turn-around for the run, discovering that she had obtained a considerable lead over me. The way she got that lead was interesting.

While treading water, Shelly's calf started to cramp very badly – so much so that she was doubled up in pain. She therefore swam over to hold on to one of the start buoys. Some nice, chivalrous guy saw her and offered to help – and he gave her a quick calf massage

to ease the pain. That helped, but he had to stop when the horn went off, and Shelly still was not in condition to start, so she just held on to the start buoy, trying to stretch her cramp out. The cramp finally eased, and she decided to start with the next wave, three minutes later. At least she could still get an open-water swim racing experience that way. With all the adrenaline she built up while waiting to start, she went on to have a great swim, bike, and run, finishing second in her age group, way ahead of me. So all is not lost if you cramp at the start, especially if you can find someone to give you a massage.

How did I fail to see Shelly pass me? It turns out that I had a bike crash after missing a sharp turn at the bottom of a hill. I had flown off the road into a bush and took some time disentangling myself and my bike from the branches. I was scratched up a bit but not seriously hurt, and so I kept racing. It was while I was in the bush that Shelly had gone by me, but she didn't realize that it was me, among others, who had crashed at that spot. Thus, we both missed out on opportunities to help each other out during that race. I guess that's what happens when you get highly focused on your own race. P.B.

Chain-reaction Cramping

In the first half-ironman I ever did in White Lake, North Carolina, I was having a slow, but relaxed, swim, taking advantage of the buoyancy of my wetsuit, when at about a quarter mile from the swim exit the cramps hit. First, it was the arches of my feet, but that subsided as I tried to flutter my feet a little more. Yet a few seconds later my calves started to seize and that brought tears to my eyes and caused me to stop, contemplating how I could signal one of the course monitors to come help me. Fortunately, the wetsuit kept me floating and as I relaxed a bit the calves released somewhat and I was able to swim slowly toward the exit without any help. Still, as I started to climb the exit ladder, both of my quads seized up and someone had to help pull me out of the water. I staggered through the transition, somehow got my wetsuit off, and eventually finished the race with some really sore quads and calves. This whole experience took a ton out of me and this is the only race I've ever done where I ended up in the medical tent afterword. The saline IV they gave me really helped! P.B.

Serious cramping during the swim can knock you out of a race or create sore muscles that will not perform optimally later in the race. Unfortunately, there is no scientific consensus on how to prevent these cramps, and there is no real easy solution about how to deal with them once they begin. Carefully-done research on the effects of hydrating and/or consuming electrolytes has not found that they make a significant difference in preventing cramps, although we know dozens of athletes and coaches who believe that a deficiency of either can cause cramps. About the only thing that seems to hold up in research as a cramp-prevention strategy is training your muscles to experience the stress they endure on race day during your training -- and not to go faster or dramatically longer during a race than you did in training. Post-workout stretching and other efforts to build flexibility might also help in cramp prevention, but on the day of a race the warm-up should include dynamic movements and muscle activation routines, but not static stretching. You don't want to stretch muscles pre-race in ways that might cause them to react with spasms or contractions!

If the cramping starts while in the water, our best advice is to do everything you can to stay calm and try to relax the cramping muscle(s). Slow your pace and try to a very light kick for stability. This is easier to do in a wetsuit. For some people, stretching the muscle in the opposite direction from which it is pulling – if you can do this while floating in the water – can help, but this can also risk aggravating the cramp even more for others. So, relaxing with deep breaths and not panicking are probably the best medicine. Think about trying some yoga breathing in moments like this.

Tip Ten: Practicing race situations, efforts, and paces will help you learn how to deal with cramps and sometimes even reduce their number and intensity.

Challenging Swim Exits

Rocky Beach

For several years, there was a Providence, RI Ironman 70.3, and one year they started out with an ocean swim. I had come the day before and practiced swimming on the course, but I made the mistake of just swimming near the swim start, and not testing out the swim exit. On the day of the race, the water was very rough and they even gave competitors the option of skipping the swim and doing a duathlon instead. But I felt confident I could handle the waves – in part because wearing a wetsuit and having salt water gave me more buoyancy – so I went ahead with it. As I rode the waves in and started to stand up to come out of the water, I peaked at my watch and saw that I had done my fastest time ever for a half-ironman swim, so I felt I had made the right decision to compete. But at that moment, I realized that the part of the beach that I had been carried to near the swim exit chute had all kinds of sharp rocks and hard stones at the bottom, and I cut and bruised my feet badly as I tried to make my way to transition. This didn't affect me too much on the subsequent bike ride, but when I hit the run, my feet were killing me, and I ended up walking a lot, which really affected my run time. Who knows what kind of race I would have had if I had scouted the swim exit and figured out which part of the beach would avoid the rocks? P.B.

Tip Eleven: Scout the swim exit and keep swimming in the race until your hand touches the bottom while swimming normally.

Conducting a pre-race inspection of the swim exit should not be overlooked. Consider what path you should take through the exit to avoid dangerous or slow footing. Develop a plan about how far you will swim before standing or walking, recognizing that as long as the water is not too shallow, you will probably move faster by swimming. It's often comical to watch people trying to run out of the water too early while fighting the water, meanwhile losing the gains they had made swimming as they get passed by someone swimming smoothly until their hand touches the bottom of the lake. That way, the water will be below your knees and you can swing your feet above the water while running.

Also, see if you will have to climb a ladder or ramp – and whether you will need to rely on a race volunteer to help pull you out of the water. If possible, practice any ladder or ramp ascent beforehand, so that you are prepared for the extra oomph you will need to get you out of the water. If the water is very cold, remember that your feet and hands may be numb, adding to the difficulty of climbing out of the water and getting your footing – so, again, practice can help.

Frozen Stiff

Coming out of the icy cold water at the 2012 World Championships in Auckland, New Zealand, I couldn't feel my feet and a volunteer missed grabbing me, so I fell flat on my face on the exit ramp, bruising myself up for the rest of the race. Perhaps more practice would have helped, but I'm not sure. P.B.

Swimming Follies

I have a handful of other examples to share to hopefully help you avoid problems in your own experiences. First, beware of floating debris. I was in the middle of a swim during a race when I got stunned as I ran face-first into a log as I went to sight. My goggles snapped in half and I thought for sure that I had broken my nose as it hurt like crazy and I could taste the blood. Fortunately, I was able to finish the swim and my nose wasn't broken, but that was one swim that I won't soon forget! Secondly, be careful where you step when getting into the water. At one national championship race in Louisiana at least one person that I know of lost their timing chip when they stepped into the muck and duck poop getting into the water. It literally sucked it right off of their ankle. You could hear everyone grunting trying to walk, it would have been much better to just wade in with your feet up behind you!

Another time, I coached a guy for several swim lessons to get him ready for his first triathlon. He was basically starting from scratch, but the race was only a 250 yard pool swim and we were able to build him up to where he should have been able to do that without issue. But, as I was spectating the race, someone came over and said that I had to see what he was doing. It ends up that the pool had no deep end and he got really nervous before the start of the race. So, he ended up walking the entire 250 yards in the pool!

You'll likely start to notice a trend with some of my stories in that I have injured myself in so many ways it's not funny. After displacing my elbow one year, I really wanted to do an upcoming race and pleaded with my orthopedic to see if I could somehow race. His answer was perfect, it would hurt a lot and swimming would be tough, but I wouldn't do any more damage than was already done. Sold! Well, he was right, of course. Swimming was excruciating. I ended up swimming with my left arm only and letting my right arm just go in short motions next to my side. However, the bike was okay as long as I left everything sit still in the aerobars and I was able to hold my arm close to my chest when I ran. Probably because I was so focused on the pain in the elbow, I ended up with a pretty good race and winning prize money for the first time. But, every muscle on the left side of my body was so sore I couldn't move it for days afterwards!

Finally, this is something that I imagine not many people have had happen to them. I was coaching a masters swim class, when one of my swimmers, who was pregnant, calmly got out of the pool, went to the locker room and left. I didn't think too much of it until she told me a couple of weeks later that she had actually gone into labor during the swim workout and delivered her daughter a short time later! D.W.

Applying the PREPARE Approach

The **PREPARE** acronym clearly applies to the Swim portion of a triathlon. You need to **Plan** for how you will warm up, line up, breathe, sight, stay on course, and exit. Contingency plans should be developed just in case you can't line up where you want or if you cramp or lose your bearings because of rough water, foggy goggles, or pushy competitors. Having a plan will help you approach the race more calmly and confidently.

It is clearly desirable to **Rehearse** how you will swim the course, getting used to the temperature, sighting, sun position, entry footing, exit footing, and so forth. We highly recommend doing a practice swim on the course the morning before a race, especially for important ones, if at all possible, and at the time you'll be starting the race. Above all, it is valuable to have done many swim workouts that simulate what the race experience will be like. Get accustomed to swimming close to other swimmers, perhaps by swimming 3 or 4 people side by side in a lane or doing some intensive work drafting other people. Also, practice sighting frequently and breathing to either side in case the conditions require you to sight more often or breathe to your less comfortable side. Doing some of this practice in open water rather than in a pool can pay dividends. You want to become experienced at swimming for long periods without pushing off a wall on a regular basis. Finally, get used to swimming hard, with an elevated heart rate, for at least as long as you will be required to swim in the race. This helps you train your muscles to avoid cramping after high intensity effort for an extended period.

Remember to **Execute** your plan for the swim, and don't let the chaos and crowding of the swim start lead you to make a spur of the moment decision to do something radically different in terms of starting position, pacing, breathing direction, or exit plan, or push you to mistakes due to frustration. At the same time, you want to be flexible enough to change to a contingency plan if the sun is brighter, the waves are higher, the current is stronger, the goggles are foggier, or the sighting is more difficult than you anticipated. It helps to think through all these contingencies before the race. That way you have various options that you can execute as needed.

Being willing to **Persist** no matter what goes wrong in the swim is really important. Having a problem at the start of a race can be discouraging and it can lead to you wanting to pack it in and save yourself for another day. Getting goggles knocked off, missing a turn, encountering a stiff current, or getting a cramp can set you back minutes in a race, but they don't have to end your day. The swim is the shortest portion of any triathlon. If the race is long enough, a strong bike and run can usually still be used to make up what was lost on the swim. And even if the deficit is too large to make up, the bike and run can be embraced as great practice sessions for the next race.

Don't forget to **Analyze**, post-race, what caused any problems during the swim. Were your problems mainly caused by faulty planning about positioning and strategy, or were the problems mainly a result of poor preparation – or by a combination of both? Was your stroke different in this race than it normally is during workouts, something that happens to the best of us in the heat of the moment, and was someone able to observe this for you? Or, was it simply a matter of bad luck or bad weather? Do your best to figure this out and **Revise** your preparation and plan for the next race accordingly.

Once you've gone through all this analysis and revised planning, commit to continuing to **Enjoy** swimming and not seeing it as something that involves tedious, solitary, exhausting training and anxiety-producing racing. Try to make it fun and social, adding unusual sets and workouts to keep it interesting. Sticking with swimming can pay dividends for your overall fitness and health, and it can provide great training for improving your biking and running, as it builds your endurance and core strength. Swim with a masters group or other training group to add a social dimension to your swim training, and that should increase your enjoyment of this great form of exercise.

4 – T1

T1, or the transition from the swim to the bike portion of the race, is probably the most under-appreciated and biggest cause of lost time in triathlon. Being quick through the transition can gain you several places against your competition, whereas a slow transition can negate gains made in the swim, bike, or run. Our rule is that if you spend more than roughly 7 seconds actually at your rack then you're wasting time! It's more than worth it to practice this aspect of the race.

Unzip-able Zipper

Even after enduring the sub-60 degree temperature and the filthiness of the Danube River, I was pumped up exiting the water at the 2012 World Age-Group Sprint Triathlon Championships in Budapest, Hungary. I had done a mistake-free swim and was coming out of the water only a few steps behind one of my friends, who normally is a faster swimmer than I. I reached behind myself to grab the string on my wetsuit, so I could start to remove it before getting to my transition spot, and I gave it a hard yank, as I normally do. But this time the zipper somehow got stuck on a piece of neoprene next to the zipper track and it wouldn't budge. A guy behind me on the exit path very considerately tried to help me get it unstuck, but it still wouldn't budge. So I ran to my transition spot thinking I might have to do the whole race with my wetsuit on—which might not have been that bad since it was raining cats and dogs that day. However, when I got to my bike, I managed to very slowly slide myself out of the opening at the top of the suit, ripping the suit in the process. This took about five minutes longer than it normally would, and it left me way behind my time goal for the race. But at least it gave me an excuse to go out and buy a new, more buoyant wetsuit with a better zipper mechanism! P.B.

Revealing Too Much

If you want a good laugh, spectate around the first transition during a wetsuit legal triathlon and watch the athletes trying to navigate their way out of their wetsuits. It's hilarious! To avoid being laughed at, it's always a good idea to practice before the actual race . . . well, almost always.

A fellow coach offered an open water clinic, which included tips and practice for taking off the wetsuit, the day before a big local race. It was well-attended and offered many great insights. Among these is to have the top of the wetsuit off so that it's down to your waist when you get to your bike in the transition area. Once there, you should take your thumbs on either side and, in one fell swoop, push the wetsuit down until your hands are at or near your ankles. If done correctly this will put the legs of the wetsuit below your knees making it easier to take off during the next step. Most people don't do this, though, and instead struggle and wiggle inch-by-inch to try to get the legs out of the wetsuit. Okay, definitely something the group should practice at the end of an open water swim practice.

Another female friend of mine participated in this clinic along with a number of other athletes racing the next day. My friend was taken by surprise, however, when another woman ran over to her right after her practice wetsuit removal. The woman quickly held out a towel and stood in front of her, and this is when my friend realized that she had grabbed a bit more than just her wetsuit with her thumbs - her bottoms were also down past her knees! And to make matters worse, she decided to sit down on the ground right away so she wouldn't be as visible to others – and lo and behold she sat down right on an anthill of biting fireants!

Lesson: wear a one-piece suit under a wetsuit; or if you prefer a two-piece, be certain to not grab onto your bottoms! D.W.

Tip One: Practice putting your wetsuit on and, more importantly, trying to take it off quickly.

Tip Two: Have your transition laid out as efficiently as possible. Helmet upside down with straps out, glasses open and in the helmet, number belt under the running shoes so you can easily grab it on the way out, and cycling shoes in the clips if you can.

In addition to getting your bearings and balance, and switching from using your swimming muscles to your running (and then biking) muscles, all kinds of other challenges can arise in the first transition. We have observed or personally experienced problems in these areas:

· Running barefoot on difficult surfaces

· Finding your bike

· Wetsuit removal

· Putting on helmets, shoes, race number, etc.

· Wheeling out your bike

· Mounting your bike

Mistakes or delays in completing any of these tasks can cost you valuable time, but perhaps more importantly, it can frustrate or discourage you and drain energy that can keep you from performing your best later in the race. Minimizing mistakes in T1 can get you pumped up and give you momentum for doing better on the bike and run. Here are some mistakes we have seen under each heading, along with ideas on how to PREPARE to avoid them.

Running Barefoot on Difficult Surfaces

Lost Shoes

The Escape from Alcatraz Triathlon was a race that had been on my bucket list since I started racing many years ago. So, when my wife and I finally got into the race, I was ecstatic. Unfortunately, I had a fairly painful leg injury heading into it. I figured that I could get through the run and fight through the pain as I had managed to do a couple of times leading up to the race, but I was concerned about the long transition between the swim and bike. With a start being from a boat floating in the Bay near Alcatraz, a long run to the bike, and complicated transition areas, it is a big set-up process for the race directors. You were able to put a pair of shoes onto a truck that would be available for you out of the water, so I decided to put out the same shoes that I planned on using for the run as I couldn't really run without shoes that far on my damaged leg.

I ended up having a really good swim, coming out near the front of the race, and was excited to see what I could do in the next legs. However, as I got through the beach, I could not find my shoes at the designated spot, or anywhere else for that matter. Considering my leg issues, I really didn't want to risk running in my bare feet on the concrete, so I spent a LOT of time looking and having volunteers search as well. My wife even came out of the water and saw me looking around, and she kindly offered to help me look, confidently saying that "we'll find them." But I told her to continue her race. I eventually decided to walk to the bike and just enjoy the scenic ride knowing that I wouldn't be able to do the run portion. On my way out, I just happened to mention to a volunteer my situation and asked if they could put my shoes next to my bike rack if they found them. Interestingly, I thoroughly enjoyed that bike ride now that the pressure was off. The scenery was fantastic and I spent the ride taking everything in. I coasted into T2 fully expecting that my race was over. I walked over to my number on the rack and didn't even notice until I was taking my helmet off that they actually HAD found my shoes and even put them at my bike rack spot! It was a great feeling and in my excitement I even ran out without putting on my race number. Again, I just cruised through the amazing run and it was so much fun. I didn't even know who to thank after the race, but sent a nice letter afterwards. Although it was not a race where I placed well or raced fast, it was one of my favorite race days ever. D.W.

Tip Three: Don't let a screw-up keep you from enjoying the day!

Ouch – What's Sticking in my Feet?

We have competed in White Lake, NC many times, in races of all different distances. The lake itself is very clean and nice, although occasionally it can get choppy. You exit the swim on a wooden dock and run about 100 yards on that dock to a grassy path that takes you to a grassy transition area. One year, there were all kinds of prickly little balls embedded in the grass, and it tore up our feet pretty badly, slowing us down on the bike and run. Ever since then, whenever we race there we scout the grass conditions very carefully before the race. If the sticky things are there, we put either running shoes or a pair of Crocs on the dock by the exit, and then we run to our transition spot in them. The few seconds it takes to put these on our feet really are worth it! P.B.

Tip Four: Scout the run from the water to the bike to avoid potential problems.

Pre-race scouting of the path you will run from the swim exit to your transition spot is very important. Besides prickly balls, you need to watch out for roots, slippery spots, holes, steps, sharp turns, and long stretches of concrete or other hard surfaces. If you are going to have to run a long distance on a hard surface and you have sensitive or injury-prone feet, then determine whether the race director allows you to place shoes or sandals near the swim exit and, if permitted, by all means take the time to put them on. You will probably run faster through the transition, making up for some of the lost time of putting on and taking off the foot protection. And you can save yourself from nagging injuries. We know several people who have suffered for years with foot problems because they beat up their feet running barefoot on hard surfaces.

Finding Your Bike

Ruby Red Bike

My wife, Shelly, normally flies out of the water and gains all kinds of time on her competition during T1. She is extremely adept at activating her fast-twitch running muscles. But this doesn't do her much good when she has trouble locating where her bike is racked and has to run back and forth in the transition area looking for it. So after a couple of races when finding her bike was a nightmare (and costing her trips to the podium), she decided a great way to remedy the problem was to buy a new bike. What would that do? Well, this new bike was painted a very bright, sparkly red, similar to the ruby-red slippers in the Wizard of Oz. Now, she (almost) always goes straight to her bike. P.B.

Tip Five: Find some kind of marker to help you quickly find your bike in transition.

Until recently, race directors tended to be tolerant with competitors using various aids to mark where their bikes were racked. We have seen people hang up balloons, fluorescent jackets, bright towels, or huge signs at the corners near their bikes. We have also seen people write in chalk on the ground to remind themselves where to turn. But in recent times, race directors have become pickier about people hanging or writing things to direct themselves, and therefore you need to be prepared to find your bike without such aids. Having a distinctive-colored bike can help, but if that is not possible, then perhaps you can get a distinctive-colored transition mat or towel to put on the ground next to your bike. Couple that with a careful scouting job that identifies notable trees, lampposts, garbage cans, porta-potties, or other signage that can remind you where to turn. Also, count the number of rows you must pass between the swim exit and your turn into where your bike is racked – and count out loud as you're running to that turn so that you don't turn too soon or too late. We've also seen people that 'accidentally' spill a little bit of talcum powder or something else that's not as obvious but will stand out as a marker to look out for.

Wetsuit Removal

Wriggling on the Ground

Getting out of my wetsuit has been a major challenge in numerous races, but I've had an especially hard time in cold temperatures, when my fingers have been too numb to grab my wetsuit firmly to yank it down or off. Ideally, you want to pull it down below your knees as soon as you arrive at your transition spot – assuming you have zipped the zipper down all the way – and then you should be able to step out of it (while still standing) by using both your hands and your other foot to push each leg off. But I have ended up getting stuck numerous times during this process, and a frequent outcome has been for me to fall hard on the ground with my wetsuit wrapped around my ankles, contorting my body to try to get it off. When this has happened, it has not only slowed my transition and caused me to be sore, but it has been extremely annoying to those around me, who have often had to step around my flailing body. Indeed, one of our friends took a picture of me in this position in Lausanne, Switzerland, after completing the ice-cold swim there at the World Championships. How embarrassing! P.B.

Tip Six: Practice taking the wetsuit off quickly, preferably without laying down and/or wrestling back-and-forth with it to get it down your legs.

When you wear a wetsuit during a race, there are a number of things you can do to speed the removal process – or at least make it less stressful. Making sure you have a wetsuit that is not overly tight around the calves or ankles is important, and some people even cut the bottoms of their wetsuits a little bit to make them looser around the ankles. In fact, several of the wetsuit manufacturers now intentionally make suits that can be cut off at the bottom of the calves without doing any damage to the suit or that are already designed with a higher cut above the ankle.

Lubricating your arms, calves, ankles, and feet is another important task. The lubricant can go on both the inside and the outside of the wetsuit. Some people use dedicated wetsuit lubricants like Tri-Slide and others do just fine with Body Glide, Vaseline, or even PAM (although many wetsuit manufacturers strongly recommend against using the latter two). Recently, we have taken to using Chamois Butt'r, normally used to prevent saddle sores inside your bike shorts, all over our feet and calves and have found it to work great. The reason to put it on the outside of your wetsuit around the ankles and wrists is that those areas turn inside out when you pull your suit off, so that is what will be sliding over your hands and feet.

In addition, we have also at times taken to finding places to remove our wetsuits that are not right at our crowded transition spots. This can prevent getting in people's way if we fall over. We try to find a pole or other solid structure that is just off the path through the transition, and we lean against it while stepping out of the suit. We then carry the suit around our shoulders to the transition spot and toss it on the ground next to our bike. This strategy can be very effective, as long as there are appropriate places along the way to do this and assuming there are no rules enforced by the race director that require wetsuit removal at your transition spot, which is often the case

Putting on Helmets, Shoes, etc.

Speedsuit Slip-up

I was doing the Ironman 70.3 in Florida near Disney World and came out of the water with a very disappointing swim split. Determined to make up time on the bike, I ran hard through the transition and grabbed my bike, helmet, and sunglasses, heading to the bike exit. I was just about at the mount line when I realized that I had forgotten to remove the speedsuit that I was wearing over my triathlon suit, – which given the high temperature I didn't want to be wearing during the rest of the race. So I leaned my bike up against a fence, took off my speedsuit (slowly, unfortunately), left it draped over the fence, and continued on. After the race, the speedsuit was still where I had left it, and I gathered it up. But that suit is still sitting at the bottom of my dresser, never to be worn again. I'm not sure whether I gave up on it because it really doesn't help my swimming or because I see it as a symbol of bad luck. P.B.

Backward Helmet

I once put my bike helmet on backwards and didn't really discover the mistake until T2. The bike strap felt a little tight and my view of the road was a little impaired at the top, and all this probably made me a little slower, but I didn't figure out what was wrong until it was too late. P.B.

In the heat of battle, it is easy to forget things or do something absent-minded during T1. We have seen people forget sunglasses, race number belts (in those races that require you to wear them on the bike), the application of sunscreen, the application of Body Glide or Chamois Butt'r for inside their bike shorts, and other important tasks. We have seen countless instances of people running back into transition to get their race numbers or having to stop to adjust their helmets! Take the few extra seconds to methodically check that you are ready for the next stage. If there are cold winds and temperatures, did you put on an easy-to-zip top that will slip on easily over your wet body to protect you from the cold? Certain fabrics are very hard to put on over a wet body, so pay attention to this. Did you put on socks, which is probably a good idea for races that have runs longer than 10K? We prefer thin socks made of synthetic materials, not cotton or wool. Wearing the socks that you are going to race in to the race on race morning, then leaving them open and/or rolled down a bit, will make them a little easier to get on when your feet are wet. Are your nutrition products stuffed in your uniform pockets or in a bento box or other easy-to-access container on your bike? In long races, the bike is the best time to fuel-up on nutrition, but you can't do that if you left everything back in transition. Develop and practice a routine to follow while at your transition spot so that you are less likely to forget an important task.

Two Left Feet

Few things can be as frustrating as when you cost yourself valuable time because of a mistake that you should have caught. That was the case for another client of mine during an elite draft legal race where several top young athletes were vying for their pro cards. He had a great swim and came out of the water in perfect position. He did his flying mount and got rolling with the first chase pack with just one or two people just up the road. However, when he went to put his feet in his shoes, he struggled to get his feet into them. After looking down he couldn't believe what he had done. He, somehow, managed to put the shoes on the wrong pedals! He had a choice to make. Try to ride like that, which was very uncomfortable, or lose the draft and take the time to switch the shoes. He decided to switch the shoes. He still went on to a top nine finish, but the people that were in the pack that he was riding with were all top five. Again, he handled it well realizing it was a good learning experience and something he'll be sure to never do again! D.W.

Tip Seven: Practice, practice, practice. Doing rehearsals of the transition will pay big dividends on race day. This includes practicing going full speed, doing it with wet feet, spinning before running to your bike to mimic the disorientation of getting out the water, and rehearsing the set-up.

Wheeling Out Your Bike

Tumble in the Grass

The nicest transition area I've ever experienced was located on a beautiful golf course near Pinehurst, North Carolina, the golfing Mecca. The grass felt wonderful on your bare feet, and it was great for wheeling your bike out and in, except there were some soft spots that I hadn't scouted in advance. So while wheeling my bike

out of transition, I hit one of those spots and took a tumble. My bike came down on top of me and, since I hadn't learned how important it is to wheel and mount your bike from the left side, and was wheeling it on the right side, the large chain ring put a big, painful gash into my left calf. On top of that, the tumble caused both of my brakes to lose their alignment and start to rub against the wheels – I had to stop twice in the first mile of the bike ride to fix it. P.B.

Tip Eight: Stand on the left side of your bike, opposite the gears, when running it out of transition and mounting.

Once again, the value of pre-race scouting of the transition area has to be stressed. A quick practice of wheeling-out your bike is in order, even if you have to do this slowly because of the pre-race crowding in the transition area. Pay attention to the surface and the traffic patterns that you will have to negotiate. If you plan to do the wheel-out in your bike shoes, look for places where your cleats might slip or skid. And if you plan to do the wheel-out in bare feet or socks, look for places where you might cut your feet or stub your toes. If possible, practice wheeling out your bike by just holding on to your seat with one hand and not the handlebars, since this should allow you to run faster.

<u>Mounting Your Bike</u>

Mounting Too Soon

I was heading for the bike mount line in a sprint triathlon (where fast transitions matter a lot), when the woman in front of me stopped dead in her tracks about 5 yards before the line. She was having great difficulty mounting and I made the quick decision that it would be best to stay as far away from her as possible, since I was afraid she might tip over on me or steer into me. I ran around her and, not realizing it, ended up mounting my bike a few inches before the mount line. Sure enough, at the end of the race I received a 2-minute penalty for this little maneuver. Had I been more patient or mounted a step or two later, it would have cost me a lot less than two minutes! P.B.

Both the most amusing and horrifying place to watch a triathlon is always at the mount and dismount lines. You can tell that most of these athletes have spent countless hours on their swimming, cycling, and running, but have devoted almost no time to practicing the transition. People are swerving all over the place, sliding on their shoes trying to get on or off the bike, slowing down too fast or too late, trying and failing at flying mounts, it's scary.

A careful examination of the mount line conditions is essential. Assess how crowded the line is likely to become, considering how narrow it is and how many people are in your starting wave. If you've practiced and are quick at jumping on your bike, when a bottleneck has formed at the mount line with people trying to get on their bikes, which does often happen, it will usually save you a lot of time to run past them before mounting. The extra ten feet is nothing in the grand scheme of things and then you're not stuck behind the people trying to get on or swerving all over the place.

Tip Nine: Wait until you are up to full speed before trying to put your feet in your shoes if you're mounting with your shoes already clipped in. If you try right away you'll likely be swerving all over the place because you have no momentum going forward.

Moreover, pay special attention to the grade of the road immediately after the mount line. If conditions are unlikely to be very crowded and the road is flat or downhill after the mount line, you should be able to do a "flying mount", where you get on your bike while running, that will get you rolling quickly. And if you're really good and have figured out how to secure your bike shoes to your bike (typically with rubber bands), you may be able to do that flying mount with bare feet, putting your feet in your shoes after you get moving at a fast pace. But if things are likely to be crowded and an uphill grade follows the mount line, then toss the plans for the flying mount and putting the shoes on while moving.

We have seen too many people fall over and crash into other competitors under such conditions. Remember that it's not just your own mounting skills you need to worry about, it's also the mounting skills of others that you must fear – and very few people are good at mounting at faster than a snail's pace and staying upright on an uphill grade. Be patient and save your energy for other bursts of speed later in the race!

Tip Ten: Make sure to put your bike in a relatively easy gear when racking before the race. Few things make the transition slower than trying to jump on and start out with a bike that's been left in the hardest gear!

Do As I Say, Not As I Do

You've heard us say repeatedly that you should practice your transition and, while daunting for many people, most can get the flying mount if they're willing to dedicate an hour or two to trying it. I've been coaching and doing these transitions for many, many years and pride myself on being quick between disciplines. But, I'll admit that I've had a couple of very public and embarrassing fails. The first occurred as I was demonstrating transitions to a group during a training weekend. It wasn't an issue getting on the bike, but while running with it. The front wheel hit a rock as I was running at full speed and trying to talk (i.e. not paying as much attention as I should have been). The wheel cut to the left and I tripped over my bike getting tangled in the frame and displacing my elbow in the process. Most of those participants refused to try the flying mount and shoeless dismount afterwards for some reason!

The second time was even worse. I was doing a transition clinic for the Endurance Sports Expo at Duke University in front of about 30 people. For some reason, they had me leading the class on a basketball court. Things were going well, and I had demonstrated the transitions a couple of times without issue. Then, someone asked if I could turn around and do it again. As soon as I tried to turn on the waxed surface of the basketball court it was like a slingshot throwing me down onto the floor as the wheels quickly slid out from underneath me. I crashed really hard and knew it was bad when I immediately felt like throwing up and started sweating profusely. Luckily, Monette had been there with me and I motioned for her to take over as I hobbled out of the door with as much of a smile as I could muster. It turns out that I had broken my pelvis! It was over six weeks before I could even think about running again and I still hear about it from people years later. In fact, at a youth race that we put on, a ten year old boy recognized me and pointed out to his mother as I was standing there that I was 'that guy' who fell off his bike and got hurt! D.W.

You Can't Teach and Old Dog New Tricks

Monette and I were selected to be assistant coaches for the AARP race series that was put on several years ago, and saw things we never expected, especially in transition. We held workouts, clinics, and wrote pieces to educate the participants about the sport of triathlon and what to expect during the race. However, we got quite a few people who told us that they were doing it their way because that's what they were comfortable with. That was fine, of course, because it was incredible just to see that many people getting out and participating in an event just for AARP aged folks. But, we still had to chuckle with a few of them. Several racers insisted on running into the locker room between the swim and the bike so that they could change into something more comfortable. At least a few put on pleated shorts, belts, and collared shirts! We literally saw one woman putting on makeup in the transition area. But, my favorite was one nice older woman who insisted on putting on bright red knee high boots for the bike ride. When we asked her about it, she said that the heels of the boots fit behind her pedals making her feel secure and it was the only way she was comfortable riding. I'm not sure how she came to this conclusion or how many other shoes she tried, but she raced like that and did just fine, so who am I to argue? D.W.

Applying the PREPARE Approach

The **PREPARE** acronym definitely can help you in T1. A **Plan** for how you will negotiate T1 should be developed and every step should be thought through carefully. Where will you remove your wetsuit (if necessary)? How will you make sure it slides off quickly? How will you find your bike? How will you order your equipment at your transition spot? What order will you put things on? What route will you take to the bike exit? How will you negotiate the mount line?

Then, you should **Rehearse** how you will go through T1, even if you have to do it at a slow speed because of pre-race crowding. Some things, like wetsuit removal and flying mounts, can be practiced regularly, although at first you should do the flying mounts on a soft, grassy spot to avoid becoming injured if you fall. Other things, like checking out the terrain for slippery spots, obstacles, and easy-to-miss turns, can be practiced by doing mental visualization before the race and also by doing a walk-through.

Making sure that you **Execute** your T1 plan should be a priority. Don't make spur of the moment decisions to put on (or take off) a piece of clothing, and don't try to do a flying mount at an uphill mount line just because things are less crowded than you expected.

However, unexpected things can happen in T1 and you need to **Persist** and plow through it. Obstacles that you missed during your pre-race inspection can get in your way, and other competitors can unintentionally (and occasionally intentionally) do things to slow you down. They can knock over or move your bike, spill or take your nutrition products, or scatter your helmet and sunglasses. Try not to let these unanticipated events upset you and try to make up the lost time later in the race.

It should not be too difficult to **Analyze**, post-race, what caused a T1 foul-up. If you realize that your plan was flawed, then by all means **Revise** the plan for the next race. And if the foul-up could have been prevented through more practicing of wetsuit

removal and mounting, per se, then start practicing those things more in your training.

Finally, try to **Enjoy** T1 and see it as a time to celebrate the successful completion of the swim and a fun change of pace to practices. Wave to the fans watching you transition, and try to keep a smile on your face throughout. Too many triathletes go through T1 with a scowl on their face. We have had several clients who enjoy the transitions so much they make it their goal to always be the fastest at every race.

5 – BIKING

Being the longest portion of almost all triathlons, in addition to being the one where you have to rely on a mechanical piece of equipment, there is a lot that can go wrong during the bike leg. Just when we think we've seen it all, something pops up to prove us wrong. I'm sure you'll find some of these stories amusing and surprising as well.

Throat on Fire

After having a great swim in an Olympic Distance triathlon in Pinehurst, North Carolina, I was really excited as I departed on the bike. Trying to be efficient, I reached down right away and grabbed some Endurolyte pills that I had taped to my top tube. It was a very hot day and I thought I might need the extra salt – I thought the sooner I got the pills in my system, the better. So as I popped the pills in my mouth and then reached down for my water bottle to wash them down, I promptly dropped the bottle on the ground. Well I was so thrilled by my swim that I decided I didn't want to give up the time it would take to retrieve the bottle, thinking I could hold out until about mile 15, when they were supposed to be having a water bottle hand-off. What I didn't count on was having one of the electrolyte pills getting stuck in my throat, quickly dissolving in place and burning the inside of my throat very badly. I had to go another 15 miles with a burning and gagging throat before I could cool it down with a drink. And even after that I still had trouble breathing (and biking and running). It took days before my throat went back to normal. P.B.

Tip One: Ensure that your water bottles and fuel are secure and won't fall out (or get dropped) over bumps.

So Long Sunglasses

Sometimes you just have to cut your losses. That was what went through my mind around mile 75 of the bike ride during Ironman Austria as I watched my glasses hit the road. As a prelude, I had been injured prior to the race and did very, very little training leading into the Ironman for the previous six months. But, I had always wanted to do Austria and decided that I'd at least do half of the ride – and the fact that my wife, Monette, was doing it also helped me make my mind up to give it a shot.

The course is absolutely breathtaking and, while it's a very fast course, there are a few hard climbs on the bike route. Of course, being out of shape and, I have to admit it, about 20-25 pounds heavy, my legs and lungs were screaming on the climbs. And, each one got worse and worse. However, when I came through the halfway point of the ride I decided to just keep it easy and try to finish the rest of the ride. So, onto the next loop I went without much in my legs at all. By the time I got to the last big climb on the loop, I honestly didn't know if I could make it up again! Partway up the hill I stood up to crank it a bit to get my cadence back up only to see my favorite Oakley Jawbones falling to the concrete. Those glasses aren't cheap and they were one of the few splurges that I allowed myself that year, so I have to admit that I was tempted to stop and pick them up. Actually, if it had been just about anywhere else on the course I probably would have. But, I didn't see myself being able to get back on the bike, clipped in, and spinning because the hill was just too steep. The decision was made – nice knowing you glasses. The race just became even more expensive!

What happened next, though, really took me by surprise. The spectators at Ironman Austria are fantastic; they really line the hills and are great at giving encouragement to get you up the incline. Well, a middle-aged man saw the glasses fall and yelled up to me what I think amounted to "hold on, I'll grab them for you" and ran to grab them. There was no way I could slow down any more, as I was doing everything I could to just get up the hill. I motioned to him that I didn't want to stop, so he proceeded to try to start running to catch up to me to give me the glasses. It was an amazing gesture and one I that I truly appreciated, however, it was a futile and short-lived attempt. He couldn't get up to me in the crowd and I wasn't stopping. At least he got a nice pair of sunglasses for his efforts!

Oh, by the way, and if you care, I did end up somehow finishing the Ironman with a halfway decent time and Monette really nailed it! D.W.

An Ice Skating Deer

A very memorable race occurred in Lake Placid several years ago, when they had a World Championship qualifier race there in early June. June sounds like it should be nice weather, right? Obviously, that isn't necessarily the case in Lake Placid, NY. We were scrambling to find neoprene caps, booties, and other cold weather essentials after realizing just how cold it was going to be. The race organizers decided to shorten the swim to a 500-meter distance due to the frigid water temperature, which helped a little bit. But, with it raining, and at points lightly snowing, along with the chilly water temps, it was impossible to warm up. I don't think I'll ever forget not being able to change gears on my bike because my fingers just wouldn't work and I couldn't feel the shifter.

Safety became a huge issue at this race. Monette was coming down a big hill, already riding tentatively because of the slick roads, when she was frightened half to death by a deer running from the woods on the side of the road. She didn't even have time to react when the deer jumped onto the road right in front of her. Luckily, the slick roads actually helped her out, because the startled deer didn't have time to hesitate as his legs splayed out from underneath him and he did a belly-slide across the road right before Monette passed. Catastrophe avoided! D.W.

Disasters on the bike come in all types. At worst, they can end your day and even put you in the hospital (see the opening story of this book). However unlikely, they can also lead to injury, exhaustion, and discouragement. As examples, problems can arise with:

·   Staying on course

·   Getting flat tires or other equipment failures

·   Keeping hydrated and fueled

·   Avoiding crashes and accidents

·   Avoiding penalties

Staying on Course

A Nightmare Coming True

I have had a recurring nightmare for years about getting lost while racing. Usually, it is about taking a wrong turn during a running race, and not being able to find my way back to the course and to the finish line. But a few years ago, I had a real experience with getting lost in the bike portion of a triathlon. It was in Pinehurst, North Carolina at a sprint triathlon being run by AARP, the organization for Seniors. They had launched a short-lived triathlon series around the country as a way to encourage more physical activity among the 50+ set. Unfortunately, some of their races had problems, and that probably had something to do with why the series lasted only a season.

In the Pinehurst sprint race, a big problem was the lack of well-trained volunteers on the bike course. As I approached a 5-way intersection early in the bike portion, I took the first right turn instead of the correct second one, and nobody tried to steer me where I should have been going. Since it was a pool-swim race that had people going off in 20 second intervals (rather than as a group), no one started the bike at about the same time I did that I could follow. And the two teenagers who were supposed to be directing people where to go at that intersection were busy talking to one another and I didn't really see them. After making the wrong turn and going about 5 minutes without seeing any other cyclists or volunteers – and also making some additional turns on Pinehurst's curvy and hilly roads – I realized I was lost, but I had no idea how to get back on course.

It took me another 15 minutes to find my way back to that 5-way intersection, where I promptly screamed something unmentionable at the volunteers and tried to make up the lost 20 minutes. Of course, 20 minutes is a lot in a sprint triathlon, so my race was a bust from a competitive standpoint, though I certainly engaged in plenty of physical activity that day. Moreover, I learned the importance of scouting the bike course before a race and, where necessary, asking volunteers for directions. P.B.

Tip Two: Know the course!

To state the obvious, it's hard to have a great race if you go off course. Well-managed races typically make it relatively automatic to stay on course during the biking portion. The roads are marked with chalk or paint indicating where to turn and how far you have gone. Cones are often set out to guide you through turns and narrow sections, and police and volunteers are stationed at intersections to wave you in the correct direction with their arms or flags. These people should also warn you where you need to slow down or be careful because of approaching potholes, rough or slick pavement, steep hills, and dismount lines. So using all this help should make staying on course a piece of cake.

The problem is that some races have slip-ups in providing directional guidance. Rain can wash away the markings on the ground, and volunteers or police can be poorly trained or even fail to show up in the first place. Race directors for triathlons face enormous challenges, and sometimes they can't take care of everything.

In the Lead

Being a decent swimmer and cyclist, I've found myself lucky enough to be at the front of quite a few races. You would think this is a good thing, and, of course, it generally is. But, I can't tell you how many times I've had issues because of that as well. There have been numerous near misses with cars, missed turns, missed bottle hand-offs due to volunteers or cops not being ready for someone yet, and so on. It's a thrill to be behind the lead vehicle, but sometimes their attention wavers and I've had to, more than once, yell to them to pick it up or, once, even pass them and signal for them to get further ahead of me (I realize that was probably not the best idea, but when you're in the middle of a race it's not fun being slowed down, especially by the lead car!). Near misses have happened with cars turning onto the course, pulling out of driveways, and when cops at intersections aren't quite ready and try to stop cars at the last second as I'm coming up to it. That's also the same reason I've missed a couple of turns in races. As I said, it's always awesome being in front, but I've learned to constantly be in the moment, pay attention, and know the signage and course as best as I can in advance. D.W.

To reduce the chances of going off course, whenever feasible, it pays to ride the bike course on your own bike prior to the start of a race. You can learn the turns, spot the potholes, test the hills, and estimate how to pace yourself. However, often a practice ride is not feasible. The town officials or police may not allow competitors on the bike course in the days before a race, wanting to avoid traffic problems or bike accidents. Or your travel plans may not allow you to have the time to ride the course. Moreover, you probably don't want to be doing a 40k ride or longer a day or two before a race. Save your legs! Ride a little bit of the course if you are allowed to and have the time, but do this just to help you visualize what the bike start and the bike finish or a particularly challenging or tricky section will be like.

If a practice ride on the bike course is not possible or appropriate in the days before a race, and you haven't been able to ride the course at some other earlier time, there are a few other ideas we can share. It pays to study the course maps, paying particular attention to sharp turns, steep hills, what mile-marker the water-bottle handoffs will be, and how the entry and exit to the course will work. Some bigger races have videos of the bike course and these can be very helpful to watch. Finally, of course, there is the option of riding the course in a car, which is fairly often the only option but allows you to observe the major features of the course without wearing out your legs.

If after doing any (or all) of these things, you still find yourself confused about course directions, don't be one of those macho people who hate asking others for travel guidance. Even if you are already on your bike in the middle of the race, slow down and yell over to another rider or to the course volunteers asking them "Which way?" It is better to lose a few seconds doing this than to head off in the wrong direction.

Count Your Laps

Some bike courses, especially in bigger cities, have to get their miles by doing multiple laps. This was the case at the World Championships in Vancouver where there were four laps to complete before starting the run. One of my clients, who happened to be a very good runner, was close to the lead for her age group when she turned into the transition area after only three bike laps. Having not realized her mistake until she was ready to start the run, her chances of a top finish were dashed. We have since seen this happen several other times. Pay attention and find a way that will help you count your laps! D.W.

Tip Three: Pay attention, especially as you fatigue.

Getting Flat Tires or Other Equipment Failures

Riding on a Flat Tire

Being from the Pittsburgh area, I was over the moon when they started holding a triathlon right downtown on a weekend that I could come up and my family could come cheer me on. It's a beautiful setting for a triathlon and I was really excited when I was in the lead of the bike half way through as we rode past the stadiums. I looked over and saw my parents, gave them a wave and thumbs up, and proceeded to ride right over a broken bottle! I knew it immediately as the air quickly left the rear tire and I stopped and got off of my bike down the road figuring my race was over. It was a very last-minute decision to race and I didn't even have an extra tube with me.

However, when I got off of the bike the official on a motorcycle had just pulled up behind me and said "what are you doing? You have at least a six-minute lead!" For some reason, I listened to him and got back on my bike to ride some of the scariest 12 miles of my life. I was literally skidding down the hills riding my brakes. How I managed to finish the ride, I have no idea but I did. My legs were DEAD, though, when I finished the bike, still in first I might add, but was passed on the run as I really struggled to finish in second. It wasn't until I went to pick up my bike that I realized a couple of other important details. 1) I had destroyed the rear 808 wheel that I had borrowed from my wife - oops! and 2) the wheel had bent so much that I couldn't even turn it one revolution without it stopping. No wonder my legs were dead - and I would be sore for days afterwards. Another example of a bad idea (and expensive one), but one that makes for another interesting lesson! D.W.

The Infamous Kona Sun

Racing in Kona was a dream for me from the first time I saw the Ironman coverage on TV. I patiently waited nine years until I did my first Ironman race and was thrilled beyond anything when I qualified the following year.

That season, I trained really well but ended up with a seriously messed up hip after finding out I had bad osteoporosis. There was no way I wasn't going to participate in Kona, though, and I was in really good swimming and cycling shape. It was incredible how much could go wrong in one day, though! This was back when the pros started at the same time as the age-groupers, just with something like a 50 yard head start. I had a good swim, 51.26 if I remember correctly, catching up to many of the pros and coming out of the water top 40 overall and with many of the race favorites. I started with the likes of Jurgen Zack, Steve Larson, and a few other big names. I was in really good bike fitness so I wanted to see how well I could hold on, but literally at mile one of the ride while riding with Steve Larson the cable to my front derailleur broke. I stopped four times to try to fix it and the bike support vehicle also tried to help, but nothing could be done about it. So, I was stuck in my easiest few gears for 111 miles! I just decided to do what I could and have fun with it. I felt like I was riding a little kid's bike and spinning the pedals crazy fast, but that's all I could do. I didn't realize until after the race that I had pushed the brake lever over so that it was lightly rubbing on my wheel as well. The rubber was well worn on that one side! But, I rode much of the course right with Natascha Badmann, so that was still fun. Of course, that fried my legs because I wasn't used to spinning like that, making my run even tougher than it would have been.

The run was hard from the start, and it was HOT. However, I was really suffering a lot worse than I had remotely expected. I felt like I was on fire and just had no energy. Again, I didn't realize it until later that in my excitement and haste in T1 that I ran right past the volunteers putting sunscreen on people and rode the entire 112 miles in the brutal Kona sun without any protection. To make a long story short, I did a mix of slow jogging and walking but did finish the race. Seconds after finishing, though, I threw up, fell to the ground, and had to be carried to the medical tent. Ouch, everything hurt! I had second degree burns with blisters all over my back and had to have at least two bags of fluids. To make matters worse, my feet had gotten incredibly torn up with the hot slog on the pavement and pouring water on myself. It took a long time to recover, but it's all about having fun and making the most of the day. I can say that I did that and have a good story to tell to go along with it! D.W.

We have stressed several times how important it is to check your bike over carefully before the race. Tighten everything down so that nothing is slipping, rubbing, or rattling. If rough or wet pavement is in the offing, lower your tire pressure a bit to around 100 psi or less (if you have wide tires), and that should help reduce the chances of a blowout, while also improving your traction. If it looks like it is going to be really windy, swap out your aero wheels for ones that will be more stable. Still, all kinds of things can go wrong – a pothole or speed bump that you didn't scout in advance could send you flying and/or flatten a tire. Or a chain could get dropped while switching gears on an uphill, leaving you pedaling air or, worse, leaving you unable to pedal at all because your chain got stuck between the chain rings and the bike frame.

Chain Troubles

A stuck chain slowed me down at the World Championships in Auckland, New Zealand. I had to flip over my bike to rest it on its seat, pull the chain with all my might to extract it from its stuck position (cutting up my hand), and then re-engage it back on the small chain ring – losing about 2 minutes in the process. P.B.

Tip Four: If your chain falls off to the inside of the front cog, change your gearing to the big ring and the chain will usually jump back on.

Money Down The Drain

Monette was doing one of our favorite races at Glade Springs Resort in Beckley, WV when she found herself with a large lead toward the end of the bike. It's a hilly course and coming up one of the hills on the back half of the ride she suddenly found herself come to an immediate halt. Shocked, she looked down to see her front derailleur broken off and bent in several directions around her chain. Her race was finished. This particular race had a nice prize purse, so as she watched the second place female eventually ride past she realized that it was an expensive mechanical problem between the lost prize money and the expense of getting her bike fixed! D.W.

Why spend all of that time training and risk your race being ruined by something as simple as repairing a flat tire? Take a little bit of time to practice changing flats, especially if riding a clincher tire. Even the rear tire can be changed and ready to roll in well under five minutes with practice. You should also know how to quickly adjust your brakes, tighten your aerobars and stem, use the barrel adjusters to make fine adjustments with your gearing, and adjust your saddle.

Tip Five: Know how to change a tire and make other simple repairs.

If you find yourself with a flat or an equipment failure, you have two basic choices: 1) try to fix the problem with the goal of finishing the race, not expecting to set a PR if in a shorter race, although in a half or full Ironman that is certainly still possible, or 2) call it a day and save yourself for the next race. Of course, the second option can be chosen after failing at the first option. The best option for you will depend on a host of factors, such as the race distance, what your repair problem is, how much further you have to finish the bike, the type of wheels you have, the repair equipment you have carried with you or have available from a support vehicle, your ability to change a flat quickly or make other repairs, and the other races that you have on your calendar.

If the race is a sprint, you may consider calling it a day. Depending on your goals, too many people may pass you by while you are trying to fix things, and there won't be time to catch them, as there might be in longer races. But if it's all about having fun, or finishing and getting a finisher's medal is important to you, no matter what the distance might be, then, by all means, try to fix the problem. If your problem is a flat tire and there is not much mileage left on the bike course, and you have tubular tires and/or very tough rims, you could try to finish the bike portion slowly without changing the flat, knowing that you still might do some damage to the wheels. On the other hand, if you are a pro at changing flats and practiced it often, something we recommend doing in triathlon training, then replace the tube or tire as if you were in the pits of a NASCAR auto race, and head on your way.

Circus Bike

I used to ride a beam bike, one without a seat post. It was a great bike, for the most part, and I had many wonderful races on it. However, there was one issue that happened more than once, and one particular time at an unfortunate place. It was during an age group Olympic distance national championship race where I had big goals. I had come out of the water with the leaders in my age group and started the bike energized and ready to roll. Someone had other plans for me that day, though. Early in the ride I hit a pothole. Not too hard, but noticeable. And, the beam on my bike broke, causing me to be stuck in the lowest position, basically sitting just above my rear wheel. There was nothing I could do about it so I trudged on feeling like I was riding a little kid's tricycle or something! Needless to say, I didn't have the finish I had hoped. D.W.

With other kinds of equipment problems, you can only do so much. Being stuck in a single gear or having a wobbly wheel can be tolerable if the remaining distance is short and the downhills not too steep. However, broken brakes, forks, stays, crank arms, or chains will probably end your day, unless there is a support vehicle that comes along to bail you out. Quitting isn't the end of the world, as it should leave you more energy and incentive for your next race.

Keeping Hydrated and Fueled

Getting Beaten by the "Beast"

The Ironman 70.3 in St. Croix (U.S. Virgin Islands) is known for having one of the most difficult bike courses in triathlon. The volcanic island has numerous hills and mountains, including a climb at the 20-mile mark that lasts about a mile and that gets as steep as a 22% grade. They call this climb "The Beast" and it is really named appropriately. But once you get past The Beast, the remaining 36 miles have many additional steep hills and, even worse, stiff prevailing headwinds in the 15-20 mile-per-hour range to deal with for at least 20 miles. Add to all this the tropical temperatures and high humidity that often get into the nineties (for both) and you have a bike leg that can drain everything you have from you, leaving nothing for the difficult 13.1 mile run that follows.

I have entered this race several times and have enjoyed the camaraderie of all the triathletes that descend on the island for a long weekend of racing and partying. Knowing how difficult the race is, I have gone in with very modest expectations and have planned, in advance, not to even try to make it up The Beast without getting off my bike. For most competitors, it is a badge of honor to say that you made it up The Beast without dismounting. For me, I would rather walk my bike up The Beast and save my legs for the headwinds and hills that follow it. Indeed, I can almost walk up a 22% grade faster than I can ride up one.

However, even with this outlook, I was unable to get past the bike portion of this race the second time I entered it. I didn't drink enough, eat enough, put on enough sunscreen, or pace myself enough to have anything left in the tank as I entered T2. It was an especially hot, humid, and windy day, and I didn't adjust my nutrition and pacing plan to adapt to those conditions. I was burning up, both inside and out, and it just didn't seem like an intelligent thing for a man in his sixties to be doing. I remember racking my bike, throwing off my helmet, and turning to my wife, who was on the sidelines cheering me on, and saying: "I quit – it's too damn hot and I want to save myself for other races!" Interestingly, about 15 minutes later, after I had cooled down a lot, I told my wife that I felt much better and wanted to finish the race. But she talked me out of it and I'm glad she did – as I had several great races in the weeks that followed. Still, I came back to St. Croix two years later and had one of the best races of my life, finishing second in my age group and earning a slot in the Ironman 70.3 World Championships. P.B.

Tip Six: Have strategies on how to deal with various conditions on the bike.

Running on Empty

The weather for the Olympic Distance World Championships in Vancouver was less than perfect, and the water that morning was crazy. I had eaten early, as I usually do, a few hours prior to my race start. I got to the race, went through all of my pre-race rituals, then went over to the swim start with Monette, who was also competing and starting a few waves prior to mine. The water was very rough, as well as pretty cold, and as we were on our way to the start we get word that they decided to delay the start of future waves due to the conditions. After waiting a while, they finally announced that the race would resume and Monette's wave took off. However, shortly after that, they announced another delay after seeing the swimmers struggling in the water.

Monette did great, 6th out of the water in her wave, but in transition she yells to me how tough the swim was and how cold she was. Meanwhile, I continued to wait. . . and wait. I hadn't brought any nutrition with me that morning, thinking that I had enough before the race start and would be fine until I got on the bike. However, by the time they finally announced that the race would be a duathlon for the remainder of the waves, and got us organized, I was starving, as it had been about six hours since I had consumed any food! I started off okay but, as you can probably guess, I simply ran out of gas toward the end of the bike and beginning of the run. Yet another lesson learned the hard way! D.W.

For races longer than sprint distance, it is important to stay hydrated and fueled during the bike portion. Since it is much easier to digest nutrients while biking than while swimming or running, the chance to drink and eat on the bike should not be passed up. The amounts you should drink and eat are basically a matter of what your gut can handle and personal taste. We'll stay away from nutrition specifics in this book since that could be a book in and of itself, but there are a few basic principles to follow. Many of the people you see having GI issues during races, especially longer ones, have taken in too much, usually while trying to force food down to stick to a plan when their body is telling them to do otherwise. You need to consume a decent amount, which can vary widely person-to-person, but don't overdo anything – eating too many gels or drinking too much sports drink can leave you bloated, nauseous, or needing to go to the bathroom during the run (or even before). The vast majority of what you ingest should be carbohydrates, with additional electrolytes, as there is very little evidence that taking in much protein at this stage will be helpful. Some people prefer to take in their carbs and electrolytes through their drinks, using products like Infinit or Carbo-Pro (a basically tasteless powder that adds mixed carbs to your drink), Nuun or Fizzz (tablets that dissolve in liquid), and sports drinks (like Gatorade and Powerade). Others like to consume gels, chews, bars, pills, or tablets.

Tip Seven: You'll get most, if not all, of your nutrition during races on the bike, so practice fueling at race effort to find what works best.

Excuse Me, Can I Borrow That?

There is some controversy whether athletes actually need to take in additional sodium or not during endurance training and racing. I'm not going to get into that debate, except to say that it has definitely made a difference with myself and some others that I know. With experience, you can learn what the signals are for when you're low and how much you need to avoid that. But, what do you do when you can tell that you desperately need sodium, but don't have anything on you? Well, Monette came up with a good solution when this happened to her during a long ride. She stopped at a convenience store/restaurant that was on the course, walked in, and used a salt shaker from one of the tables! It worked and gave her a good pick-up to continue on with her ride. I also had another client that had dropped her salt tabs during an Ironman race. Getting to the point where she knew she needed it, she literally picked some off of the ground that someone else had dropped! D.W.

One way to make sure you keep drinking and eating is to hook up one of the many different hydration systems that allow you to keep sipping easily all through the bike ride. The liquid could be held in a container between your aero-bars, in a container attached elsewhere on your bike (e.g., the downtube), in a bladder in your bike frame (expensive!), or in a bladder on your back, and a sipping tube (with or without a bite valve) can be set up in front of your face. Depending on the length of the bike ride, you may not be able to store enough liquid between these containers and your other bottle cages, and you will have to obtain additional liquids at a bottle hand-off during the race. This will then require you to pour the liquid into the containers, sometimes having to slow down to do so – and perhaps do some adroit mixing of pills and liquids while on the move. During training, practice rides should be used to test out what your gut can tolerate and what hydration systems you can operate without crashing your bike or slowing dramatically.

Of course, some people prefer to avoid hydration systems and just sip from water bottles and eat gels and tablets. That is perfectly fine, as long as you are disciplined enough to drink and eat regularly when you don't have a bite valve or straw sticking you in the face. Many people forget to do this while competing really hard. Whatever you do, keep the ingestion at a steady pace and don't try to "load up" only at a certain portion of the bike ride. Indeed, there is research that suggests that loading up right before T2 can hurt your performance, as your body has to use energy to digest those calories as it changes between very different types of motion and it can make you feel sluggish as you switch from biking to running.

Tip Eight: Using a good drinking system, such as one that goes on or between your aerobars, can make drinking during the cycling leg easier while also reminding you to take in fluids while in the midst of racing.

But, I Read It In a Magazine...

Realizing that nutrition plays a vital role in having a successful and fun day during an Ironman race, I perused every piece of advice I could find for my first few races and tried many things. One particular article was well written and detailed how different many people's nutritional needs were on the bike and gave specific amounts for calories and carbs of several top professionals. In my youthful wisdom, I decided it would make sense to try somewhere around the upper limits of what they described and reduce on subsequent rides as needed. To make a long story short, I started at 700 calories per hour. Yes, you heard that right, 700 calories per hour. Needless to say, I got to the point where I was throwing up. The next several rides were similar as I reduced the caloric intake weekly down to more humane levels. It took a LONG time after this experiment before I could stomach another Gatorade or Powerbar as I had taken in, and forced out, so many during this time. By the way, I typically take in between 300-350 calories per hour now, mostly in liquid form! D.W.

One problem that can arise if you are conscientious about hydration on the bike is a need to pee. We have one friend that handled it this way:

A Funnel for Your Shorts

What would you do to not have to stop in a race and pee? In an Ironman event in particular, most agree that it's a good sign that you're taking in enough liquid and keeping your effort under control if you feel the need to urinate while riding. What makes this tough, though, is that it can be really hard to stop and get yourself going again, not to mention the time lost while not moving. So, then, your only other options are to hold it or let loose while you're actually still on the bike.

While I know a lot of people who are fine with the idea of peeing on the bike, it's actually a skill that many struggle with even if they decide they want to try it. Some athletes just can't relax enough to make it happen or just struggle with the idea. Then, there are those that are caught in between. They know that they should relieve themselves, don't want to stop, but really don't want to do it in their uniforms. This, obviously, creates an interesting dilemma.

A friend of mine had an interesting solution to this problem, however. He literally designed a 'funnel' that he wore in his shorts! Yes, he could open the funnel portion and use it when he had to go and the tube went down his leg and he would lift his shorts over the bottom of it so that it would flow behind him while peeing. According to him it worked great, and he went on to qualify for Kona and had an amazing race on The Big Island. So, who am I to argue with that?

I couldn't help wondering about what went through the minds of the cyclists behind him in the race, though, or if they even noticed what was happening! D.W.

Tip Nine: It's not unusual to find that you have the urge to pee, so it helps to have a plan for what you will do if the need arises. Many people, believe it or not, will urinate while coasting on their bikes.

Avoiding Crashes and Accidents

Slip Sliding Away

Rain is to be expected when traveling to London, UK, and we had plenty of it when competing in the World Championships there in September, 2013. The weather was especially nasty on the day of the sprint race, which my wife, Shelly, was doing. Since I was racing the next day in the Olympic distance event, I tried to help her out by quickly scouting her bike course while she warmed up. I ran over to see how the people who went off in waves before Shelly were handling the wet conditions, focusing on a nearby sharp turn that I had seen on the course map. I was alarmed when I saw five different people slide out and crash on that turn within a period of about 5 minutes! Things were really treacherous at that spot, and because it was a three-loop course, there were three times it had to be negotiated.

I ran back to where Shelly was queuing up for the swim start and yelled over to her what I had seen. I pleaded with her to slow down and take it easy on the bike. Well in the heat of battle my

warnings were not completely heeded. Shelly did fine on that bad turn the first time she went by, so I guess that gave her confidence that she could handle the conditions. And she also did fine on a U-turn a few miles down the road. But when she came to a roundabout where she was supposed to enter at 6 o'clock, go counter-clockwise all the way around to 9 o'clock, and then make a right to continue on, she shifted her weight off her outside right foot too soon, thinking the exit from the roundabout was at 12 o'clock. With the turn continuing on to her left, she went down and slid on the whole left side of her body for about 20 feet along the hard pavement. Her bike went sliding away on its own for at least another 10 feet. Interestingly, she may have been protected while sliding because her body was so greased up with the Chamois-Butt'r she had applied to help her get out of her wetsuit rapidly. Miraculously, after such a scary fall, she was able to immediately remount the bike and continue on without losing more than a few seconds. In fact, one guy who saw the whole thing while riding behind her yelled to her: "Jolly good show!"

Meanwhile, I was waiting for her to come near that first bad turn and was oblivious that this had happened. I thought that her first lap had taken a little longer than expected, but I didn't see any scrapes or blood on her as she went by on the next two laps, so I thought all was OK. I didn't know anything had gone wrong until I greeted her cheerfully in the finishing chute (after a 10th place finish) and she lifted up her uniform shorts to show me the terrible road rash she had gotten on her left thigh and butt. Interestingly, her high-tech uniform was not ripped or torn a bit, and it had hidden the evidence of the accident. The next day, in my Olympic Distance race, I took to heart what Shelly had experienced and was very careful where she had spilled, and I had one of my best races ever. P.B.

Tip Ten: Crashes happen. They happen quickly and you don't have much time to think, but try to have it in your head to not try to stop your fall by putting your hand out.

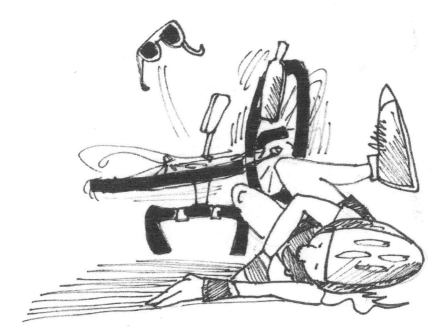

Pay Attention

Many cycling accidents can be prevented because they occur when we're tired or our attention wavers just for a fleeting moment. I had a couple of clients who got in an accident because metal poles fell off of a truck in front of them, with one of them ending up with a broken wrist. Another friend got in a very serious and scary crash when he rode full speed into the back of a bus. Personally, I once rode up to a stop light on campus behind a car. I looked down as we approached not realizing that the light had just turned yellow and the driver decided to slam the breaks to stop at the light. I didn't have enough time to react and rode into the back of him falling onto the trunk. I didn't suffer injuries, for once, and there was no damage to the car that I could see. But, there wasn't even much time to check because as I'm picking myself up he just drove off. D.W.

Tip Eleven: Practice being able to stop quickly without falling or flying over your handlebars.

Fire Fighters to the Rescue

And, what happens when you're stuck? I've had to call Monette more than once to pick me up somewhere. But, a young client had an issue where she had gotten a couple of flats and was out of tubes while in the middle of nowhere without a cell signal. Not seeing any other option, she decided to stick her thumb out and start hitchhiking. She lucked out when she eventually got a ride... in a fire truck! Being in the truck sandwiched between a couple of nice-looking fire fighters, she was loving it. To add to the experience, they even let her turn on the sirens for a bit! D.W.

We have seen and experienced all kinds of bike crashes. Some have been caused by unseen potholes and speed bumps, others by wet or icy conditions, others by going too fast on sharp turns, others by equipment problems, and others by mistakes or aggressiveness of other riders. We have also seen people crash at water-bottle handoffs and at bike mount and dismount lines (and even while practicing on a basketball court).

Pre-race scouting of the course and checking of your bike, when and where possible, can help to reduce the likelihood of crashes, as can careful, prudent riding that pays attention to the weather conditions and course features. Also, obviously, having experience riding outside in different weather conditions can make a huge difference. Watching out for packs of drafting cyclists who might sweep you off the road – which shouldn't exist if no-drafting rules are being enforced, but unfortunately still often do – can also help.

Scary Crash

We were at a World Championships in Australia where a peloton of young cyclists (illegally) surrounded an older woman, who then panicked and crashed, ending up in a hospital for several months. P.B.

Avoiding Penalties

Getting Overtaken

Here is another problem I had in a race in Pinehurst, North Carolina. In this Olympic Distance race, everything was going great. I had a fantastic swim, smooth T1, and did the whole bike feeling like I was Superman, averaging a higher speed than I had ever done in my life. I didn't drop my water bottle or fail to take enough nutrition, and I had enough in the tank to complete the hard run with an overall finishing time about 10 minutes faster than I had hoped and setting a personal record.

The only problem was that I got a 2-minute penalty for not doing the right thing when I was "overtaken" during the bike ride. My mistake was that in climbing a hill surrounded by a group of other riders, I did not drop back fast enough, after being passed, to a position at least 7 meters behind the passing rider. I knew about this rule, but 1) I didn't know there was an official on a motorcycle riding along with our group and 2) I didn't think they would enforce the rule because it was so hard to do anything other than what I did given the steepness of the hill and the crowded conditions. It was hard to reduce speed and still feel like I would make it up the hill without wobbling too much, and there was also another rider right on my tail who I didn't want to upset by slowing down. Fortunately, I still won my age group (and a nice prize). But the penalty ended up costing me a few places in my yearly ranking from USA Triathlon – something that compulsive triathletes like me pay attention to. P.B.

Yes, it is tempting to draft, pass on the right, or talk to a friend while riding (which blocks others), but doing any of these things risks getting time penalties and it can make you feel guilty for violating the social norms of triathlon besides being generally unsafe and/or unfair during a race.

Our Own Private Draft-fest

The Azalea Sprint Triathlon in Wilmington, NC is usually the first race we do every year. It has a 300 yard pool swim, where people are sent off in a time-trial start every 10 seconds, and the people who seed themselves as faster (by submitting estimated 100 yard swim times) go off first. Shelly and I had always seeded ourselves with the same time and, typically, the race director had sent us off with me right before Shelly. A few years ago, Shelly almost caught me at the end of the swim and then raced me through transition, emerging from T1 a few seconds ahead of me. I quickly caught up to her on the bike, and as I passed her I expected her to follow the rules and drop back, not really able to keep up with me. But a few hundred yards later I realized that Shelly was right on my tail, and she stayed there except for two or three times when she passed me on turns – and I passed her right back.

Realizing we were drafting and breaking the rules, I yelled to her that I thought she should stop it. But moving along at 21 miles per hour was not an especially good time to have a family debate and I couldn't succeed in persuading her to drop back. We never got caught for drafting and we both finished the 10-mile bike in one of our fastest mile-per-hour splits ever. We went on to both have solid runs and win our age groups. However, as I crossed the finish line, another competitor (from a different age group) approached me and angrily balled me out in front of many others for having drafted on the bike. He rightfully said that it was unfair and dangerous to the other riders. I apologized and agreed that he was absolutely right – I shouldn't have let myself be pulled into the drafting dance.

When Shelly finished, I asked her what she was up to and her explanation was this: "When we compete overseas, they never enforce the no-drafting rules and we're at a disadvantage, because we never practice drafting while racing. I thought this was a good opportunity to practice drafting, even if I got a penalty." I understood her rationale, but I didn't agree with it. I still feel guilty for having done this. So we don't seed ourselves together anymore, eliminating the temptation to turn the race into a draft-fest. P.B.

Tip Twelve: Learn the rules for cycling and follow them carefully.

Applying the PREPARE Approach

Pain in the Butt

The following is a race report I wrote up after doing Ironman Maryland in 2014. It shows several aspects of the PREPARE approach that we're preaching and how things can suddenly go wrong on the bike.

After doing pretty well at Ironman Brazil on very limited run volume, I wanted to give another Ironman a shot and see if I could improve on it. This is the inaugural year for Ironman Maryland with a late announcement, so it was still open and I didn't have to spend a fortune getting there. Game on. My training actually went pretty well heading into it, and although I could still only run twice a week typically, I got in several long runs and was faster than I've been in a long, long time. I was excited to see what I could do, and thought that I could go under 9:30 as my ultimate goal.

The water temperature supposedly went down the day before the race making it wetsuit legal, which I was hoping it wouldn't be, but that's okay. I hate wearing a wetsuit, so decided against it, and according to Monette was one of extremely few who didn't. But, it was definitely worth it. I felt really good on the swim, going fast but easy. There was one guy who many people seemed to know and who smoked everyone in the water, but I stuck with the front pack behind him for most of it with one or two just ahead. It was probably the easiest swim I've ever had in a race like that, where it just clicked and felt great. Unfortunately, the swim was long! I wanted to go no slower than a 54, and probably did that for 2.4 miles, but my official time was 58 minutes. When you're top 10 out of the water, you know that time is off. Several people who had done other Ironman races recently were 6+ minutes slower this time. Oh well, I didn't know that until later, though, and got ready to ride.

The first half of the bike was FUN. I passed a couple of people right out of transition and then got into a groove. The road was flat and there was no wind ... yet. I had no idea where I was, but I was COMPLETELY by myself and kept wondering where everyone was. One man was running along the course a little way into it and yelled out to me "you're about 15 back". Okay, 15th place, that's pretty good and I can try to pick people off. The problem was that I'd come up on stretches where you can see really far ahead of you and I just never saw anyone! Were they all that far ahead? I was keeping it comfortable and probably averaged around 24 mph for the first loop. The wind picked up a bit around mile 45 or so probably, but I felt great.

It was around mile 40 when someone yelled out to me that I was in 2nd place OVERALL and the first guy was 10-minutes ahead!! WHAT?! WOW, that was a shock and I was pumped. And, that explained why I hadn't seen anyone! It felt really, really good and I couldn't believe it. But, a lot can happen in an Ironman and, unfortunately, my day didn't stay perfect.

Shortly after seeing my family at mile 58, I hit something and it knocked my sensor to my speedometer into my spokes. It caused me to jerk but I managed to avoid falling or having to stop. However, in doing so I did something to my glute and it was very painful. I had to slow down quite a bit because I just couldn't push through like I normally do. To make matters worse, the wind really picked up – ugh! Bad timing. Also, I didn't have any feedback in terms of speed or distance now, except for the signs every ten miles. Ten miles can seem to take pretty long when you're in pain and have no other feedback!

I only had two other mishaps on the bike, though. I lost a full bottle of nutrition early into the ride when I bumped it on my leg and just lost the handle on it. I always plan to adapt to various situations on race day and easily accepted this and used the Perform they had on the course, even though I don't really like it. Then, at mile 80, I had run out of fluid and was really thirsty for water. But, when I got to the aid station, they weren't ready and all had their backs turned. When they finally heard me yelling for water, one guy ran out, but he handed me more Perform, which I really didn't want at that point. I only fumed about that for a few minutes before moving on. Even still, though, I didn't get passed until a guy came flying by me just after mile 80 and I amazingly still came off of the bike in 3rd overall! My ride time was a 4:47, even faster overall than Brazil, so I'll take it. One thing that I hate is that there was a pack of about 10 that had ridden together (Monette even got pictures), that wasn't far behind. They save so much energy and it's so much easier for them to run after that. Oh well, there's nothing I can do about that, so I didn't worry about it during the race.

I got a couple of oohs, though, as I almost fell when I tried to get off of my bike because my glute hurt so badly. I had to go to the bathroom, so limped over and jumped in the port-a-john as I tried to loosen up my glute and then went to change. A long-time friend was in the changing tent when I got there and he told me about the pack and that I had been passed by about ten people while going to the bathroom! And, he was right. I went from 3rd to 13th by the time I started the run.

The run started out painfully. I had to limp with my left leg almost straight for a while. I thought I was able to fake it okay, but my finisher pictures showed how much I was favoring my left leg as I was bent sideways pretty dramatically every time I landed on it.

In case you think I'm exaggerating, you can even check out the agonizing video of my attempt to start running out of the changing tent on the transition camera on the Ironman feed!

But, amazingly, I was still able to hold a decent pace for the first four miles as I tried to run as normally as I could. However, it got to be a bit too much and I was forced to slow my tempo down. I stopped looking at my watch because I didn't want to get frustrated if my pace slowed too much and wanted to trust going by feel. My second loop of three was rough. I just couldn't get into a groove and felt flat, but my leg did loosen up. Then, oddly enough, around mile 17 I started to feel good. I started to run a bit faster and passed back several people that had passed me and I felt fluid and mostly fresh again for the last loop. It was good to see that my fitness was good enough to have that happen and reaffirming after really suffering since mile 58 on the bike. I had lost a lot of time through the middle of the run and figured it would be tough to break 10 hours, but hadn't been keeping track and really didn't know. I savored the last mile, taking in the crowd and high-fiving the kids on the road. Then, I was pleasantly surprised when I saw a 9:38 on the clock as I came into view of the finish line! After feeling so rough for such a long stretch, I was pretty darn happy with that.

I ended up 7th in my age-group and 29th overall, so I dropped a lot on the run with a 3:45 split! It's a little bitter-sweet, as I had a lot more to give on the day, but at the same time, I can't complain and am definitely happy with the time and to finish another Ironman. I feel that I was in good shape coming into this one and was, amazingly, not even really sore the next morning – except for some major chaffing! D.W.

PREPARE applies to the bike leg as much as any portion of the triathlon. There is a plethora of things that you need to **Plan** for with cycling. Some of these include planning for what the course will be like and how you will deal with it. Are there steep hills that require different gearing than you normally use on your bike? Will the winds be stiff, making the use of deep-dish or disk wheels risky? Will the pavement be rough, suggesting a need to lower your tire pressure a bit? How will you deal with hydration and nutrition on the bike? Will you need to carry spare tubes, a pump, lots of food, or something to keep you warm (e.g., arm warmers)? What sunglasses will you wear? How do you want to pace yourself during the bike?

As always, it is valuable to **Rehearse** how you will handle the bike course as best you can. Try to schedule a ride of the course in the days or weeks before the race, but if that is not possible, at least ride the beginning and end of the course or drive it in a car so that the terrain becomes familiar. More importantly, practice riding the distance of the race on numerous occasions, paying special attention to seeing how your body handles the hydration and nutrition strategy that you have selected. See if you can hold a particular pace for that distance without bonking, cramping, or depleting yourself seriously.

On race day, try to **Execute** your biking plan and not let your competitive juices take over and have you push too hard or drink and eat too little (or too much). If unexpected conditions like high winds, rain, rough pavement, or crowded riding develop, try to adapt to those conditions. Stay in your aero position in the high winds and slow down with rain and rough pavement where warranted. A crowded bike course may force you to come up out of your aero position, and if you see a lot of drafting going on, you may need to back off when being overtaken.

Whether your bike split turns out slower or faster than you had hoped, **Analyze**, post-race, what seemed to explain the performance. What was outside of your control (e.g., weather, potholes) and was there something you might have done a little better (e.g., drank more, eaten more, maintained a higher or more consistent wattage or cadence)? **Revise** your plan for the next race and begin testing things like how your stomach handles certain drinks and nutrition products.

Most of all, **Enjoy** the bike leg. It is usually the portion of the race that has the most beautiful scenery and that generates the greatest feelings of exhilaration. Revel in the knowledge that you are out there doing something you love with a fascinating group of like-minded people.

6 – T2

Some people love it, some people hate it, but the transition from cycling to running, otherwise known as T2, should be a fast, simple, smooth, and efficient aspect to the race. There's really not much to do, right? Get off of your bike, run to your rack, take off your helmet, switch shoes (for most people), grab your race belt, and head out. Of course, by now you know that we'll share a few of our tales of how this could potentially not be the case. You'd be surprised at how we have found ways to screw it up!

Lost in Transition

Throughout the years, I have experienced and seen tons of crazy things during the bike to run transition. First of all, if you ever want to watch some scary moments in a triathlon, spectate at the dismount line. You will likely see many people who try to get off quickly with their bike shoes still on, slipping and sliding all over the place. Or you'll see people slamming on brakes and almost falling (if not completely falling over), athletes trying to get off while going too fast and out of control, people taking their helmets off while still slowing down, and much, much more. We've also seen countless people start the run with their helmets still on, which is always funny to see, and others have been seen running out of the wrong exit, putting their numbers on upside-down, and, more than once, knocking the bikes over like dominoes when being careless with their own bike. A few times, I've been at races with separate T1 and T2 locations where a participant's shoes didn't make it to the transition area. Twice, I've even seen spectators actually loan shoes to these athletes, although, one of these athletes I know ended up with excruciating blisters because of it!

One of my own fiascos was when I had already taken my foot out of my cycling shoes as I came to the dismount line, but then hit a speed bump that threw me off a bit and knocked my shoe off of my clips. It's always frustrating to have to try to go back and get something like that, and it can be dangerous as well. In addition, another time, I got to my bike rack only to find someone else's bike already in my spot! To avoid a penalty, you have to move their bike to put yours in the correct space, which feels like a frustrating waste of time. D.W.

Tip One: Be quick, but don't rush. Sometimes trying to gain a couple of extra seconds can cost you much more than that.

Running with a Helmet on

A friend of mine once forgot to take his helmet off in T2. He did much of the run with people looking at him funny and yelling something he couldn't understand, but he went several miles before he realized what he had done. Needless to say, he was very embarrassed when he finally recognized his mistake, and he lost some time figuring out what to do with his helmet for the rest of the race (someone volunteered to bring it to the finish line). P.B.

Tip Two: Don't forget to take off your helmet!

Rushing Way Too Much

At one major half-ironman race, they had people from each age group racking their bikes on the same rack or group of racks. As I rolled my bike to our group's rack after completing the bike portion, I didn't see any other bikes there, indicating that I was in first place at that stage. However, another competitor in my age group racked his bike a few seconds after I did – and, unfortunately, that got my competitive juices flowing. For some crazy reason, I got it in my head that, if I could exit T2 ahead of him, I would have a psychological edge for the run portion of the race. I mistakenly thought (or wished) that he would push so hard to try to catch me at the start of the run that he would blow his legs out, making it easy for me to plod along and win. So in my rush to exit T2 ahead of him, I failed to gather up all the electrolyte pills and gels I had planned to consume during the hot, humid, hilly, half-marathon run. The single gel I had with me was clearly not enough – in spite of having sports drinks to consume at the water stops – and I fought off cramping quads and calves throughout the whole run. My competitor passed me in the second mile and I couldn't even come close to staying with him. More patience and more fuel might have made it more of a contest. P.B.

The second transition can have just as many opportunities for disasters as T1. We have seen troubles in:

· Dismounting the bike

· Wheeling your bike to your transition spot

· Changing clothing and gathering up necessities for the run

Here are some stories and advice about T2.

Dismounting the Bike

Take both feet out and pedal on top of your shoes as you ride up to the dismount line before heading into the transition area. If there are a lot of curves or people, then get out of your shoes well in advance so you're not trying to do this while also having to negotiate turns and traffic. Make sure to take both feet out. We have seen countless athletes slip and fall, some badly, when trying to stop with their slippery cycling shoes still on or because one foot is still clipped in. This is much easier to learn and do than the flying mount and is at least worth giving a shot. Again, the key is to not be going too slow when trying to get your foot out of your shoes. The slower you're going, the less stable you will be.

Bare Feet Blunder

There are some athletes who are really adept at mounting and dismounting their bikes. They can do a flying mount on to their saddle off of bare feet, slipping their feet into their bike shoes while the bike is moving. They use rubber bands to hold their shoes in place as they have rolled their bike through transition. Similarly, they can do a flying dismount, taking their bare feet out of their shoes while approaching T2, pedaling a short distance with their feet resting on top of their shoes, throwing their right leg behind the saddle and then coasting with both feet balancing on the left pedal, and, finally, jumping off the bike running nearly full speed as they cross the dismount line while guiding the bike with their right hand. The pros and top amateurs all do this without any problem and it is beautiful to behold (and can also save 15 seconds or more).

But some of us old guys are too physically and mentally inflexible to do all of this. We have great difficulty moving our legs around the way you need to, and we aren't patient enough (or brave enough) to practice all this and endure the spills and mishaps that will inevitably occur while practicing, even though we would be smart enough to do these sessions on grass or another soft surface. However, the one thing I have mastered is how to take my feet out of my shoes before dismounting, although I still need to bring my bike to a full stop before gingerly swinging my leg over the saddle and then resuming the wheeling of my bike. At least having my shoes off saves me the time of removing them at my transition spot. And in many cases I can run faster through transition in bare feet than I can in bike shoes.

The removal of my feet from the shoes while riding has usually served me well, but not always. There was a sprint triathlon at the beach in Falmouth, Massachusetts, which had a short (9 mile) and very crowded bike leg, where this strategy failed me. The race attracts a lot of novices and it has a confusing bike route for the last mile, so people are all over the road and not necessarily staying to the right side. I removed my feet from my shoes much too soon, and with my feet on top of the shoes instead of inside them, I couldn't make the quick acceleration moves I needed to do to weave my way through all the traffic effectively. My feet would go flying off the shoes and pedals if I mashed down too hard on them. A friend of mine went rapidly by me at this stage, even though I had managed to stay ahead of him until that point. I estimate that this maneuver may have cost me more than a minute, as I was slowed almost to a crawl and my transition run wasn't really any faster using bare feet. That was a lot of time to lose in a short sprint triathlon. P.B.

Tip Three: It is typically much faster and not too difficult to learn to take your feet out of your shoes before getting off of your bike.

We have suggested earlier that it is a good idea to do a practice ride of the end of the bike course. Again, consider how crowded, hilly, and bumpy the last quarter mile will be, and pay special attention to where the dismount line is located. Above all, evaluate whether the conditions are right to remove your feet from your shoes before the dismount. If you decide to do this, plan where you want to do the removal while riding and think about where you want to brake and dismount. Decide what kind of dismount you want to do, and by all means don't try anything you've never practiced before. T2 is not the place to do your first running dismount.

Wheeling Your Bike to Your Transition Spot

Stuck in the Muck

There was a race we did in the outskirts of Charlotte, North Carolina which had a dismount line that was followed by a transition run that went through a downhill wooded path first before getting to where the bikes were racked. It had been very wet and rainy and the path was a mudhole. They put a carpet down over it, but that didn't really help and only created something akin to a waterslide, which people tumbled down holding on to their bikes. I observed this situation before going off, so I had decided that the best strategy would be to walk in the muck on either side of the carpet. This worked fine except for one problem – my bike (and feet) got stuck in the muck. Besides losing lots of time trying to extract my bike and feet, I also had to ditch my shoes (which I had left on) and leave them in the muck until after the race. P.B.

Walking the route from the dismount line to your transition spot should not be overlooked before the race. You want to observe where roots, rocks, mudholes, potholes, or other obstacles might trip you up. Remember that, if you plan to remove your feet from your shoes while you are on the bike, your shoes could scrape along the ground or hit obstacles while you are wheeling your bike. In addition, look for signs, plants, or structures that will remind you where to turn, and assess how crowded things might be when you rack your bike. Decide which side of your racked bike you want to use to put on your running shoes, setting up your transition spot accordingly. If you think you will need to sit down or kneel down to put on your running shoes, make sure there is a place to do this that won't lead to you being run over by someone wheeling their bike.

Tip Four: As in T1, it's best to run while holding onto your bike with one hand, preferably on the saddle.

Just like in the first transition, it is best to run your bike with one hand. The best way to do this is to grab the saddle with your right hand shortly after jumping off. This allows you to open up and run pretty much normally without as much risk of bashing your shins on the pedals as if you were running with two hands holding the bike. Also, it takes a little bit of practice, but using the saddle instead of the handlebar stem gives you a bit more speed and control, as well.

Just remember that if the racks are singularly numbered that your bike has to have most of the bike facing on the side of the rack that has your number. You'd be shocked how often people

get penalties or have to re-rack for not doing this correctly.

Pay attention to the specific rules for what is permissible in transition for the particular race. Some of the international competitions we have done require you to rack your bike by its seat, facing out, and do not permit using any stools or paint buckets to sit on while changing shoes. Other races allow you to rack your bike by either the seat or the bullhorns and they find it totally acceptable to leave a stool or an upside down paint can in transition to sit on. Some races have used "racks" which only hold on to the bottom of a wheel (and they may require that it be the rear wheel or the front wheel), and other races have put strict limits on how wide your transition spot can be or on how far the spot can extend into an aisle. Don't test these limits or you will risk disqualification or a stiff time penalty.

Tip Five: Usually, the fastest way to rack your bike is by the saddle for T1 and by the brakes/handlebars in T2.

Changing Clothing and Gathering Up Necessities for the Run

Keep It Buckled

At her first international race in Australia, Shelly finished the bike leg among the leaders. She dismounted her bike running at full speed and, trying to be efficient, unhooked her bike helmet with one hand while she was wheeling her bike with the other. Well as soon as she got to her transition spot, an official ran over to her and told her that she had to stand still for 30 seconds. Not understanding what was going on as several of her competitors passed her (never to be caught), she asked: "Did I do something wrong?" It turns out she violated one of the cardinal rules of triathlon, which is enforced all over the world: You cannot unhook your bike helmet until your bike is racked! She took her penalty, but had to get in the last word with the official, which was: "Why are you spending your time penalizing little old ladies for unbuckling their helmets a few seconds too soon, while you let all those young guys draft on their bikes, which is dangerous?" P.B.

Tip Six: Don't unbuckle your helmet until your bike is racked. It's dangerous and illegal in triathlons!

Using the Wrong Laces

After moving to NC for grad school, I started to train a little more seriously for triathlon. I really didn't know how I stacked up against the strong local competition as I entered into my first race season. Since I had just finished a collegiate swimming career, I was able to come out of the water in the lead in my first race. Surprisingly, to me at least, I held onto that lead as I entered T2 off of the bike. However, still being somewhat new to trying to go fast, I came out of the second transition in 4th place after sitting down to tie my shoes and taking my time getting everything situated for the run. The guys at the end of the race ragged me about it, but were also nice enough to suggest that I go straight to the local running store to pick up a pair of EZ laces! D.W.

Once you have unbuckled and removed your helmet, you want to shed bike shoes and unneeded clothing as rapidly as possible. If you removed your feet from your shoes while still on the bike, then they will stay on the bike, obviously. However, don't forget to remove any extra jackets, arm warmers, headbands, or the like, since the temperature will often be warmer during the run and you won't want to have to carry clothes or toss them (risking a penalty) during the run. Slip your feet into your running shoes, using elasticized laces that will stretch out and then contract around your feet. If you are doing a long race and sun exposure could be a problem, then make sure to spray yourself with some sun block. Grab your 1) hat or visor (if you like to wear one of them), 2) any pills, tablets, or gels you want to consume during the run (to obtain the carbs and salt you will need in longer races), 3) your race belt with your race number, and head out toward the run start.

Tip Seven: Use elastic laces or something similar so that you can quickly get into your shoes with a comfortable fit without having to tie your laces.

Gu in My Shoe

There was a race in Wilmington, North Carolina where I slipped on my running shoes more quickly than usual and then headed out on the run course. The problem was that something was sticking me in the heel while I was running. It turns out that I had left a packet of Gu in my shoe. I had put it in my shoe with the intention of grabbing it and eating it at the start of the run. But I forgot that it was there. Stopping to remove it cost me some time, and my foot hurt for a while after. I'm just glad that the Gu didn't burst and get all over the inside of my shoe! P.B.

Many people will put the gels, pills, or other simple things that they want for the run inside their running shoes for two reasons; so that they won't forget it in the haste of T2, and so that it doesn't get displaced while others race through transition. This can be fine, although we have ourselves both tried to put on our shoes only to realize that we left something inside of them! Another option is to have your run food in a bento box, taped to your tube, or in some other way attached to your bike where you can easily get to it. Then, you just put it in your jersey pockets, under the leg of your shorts, or wherever else you can put it so that it'll already be on your person when you start the run. This way it'll be sure to not slow you down at all, as long as you remember to grab it, that is.

Tip Eight: Put your fuel for the run somewhere where you'll remember it.

Of course, there are race belts that allow you to store gels and pills in zippered pockets or elasticized holders. But these belts only make sense if the race does not require that you wear your race number on your body during the bike portion, since you can avoid carrying extra weight during the bike ride. But a word of warning is in order here. We can't tell you how many times we have dropped gels and pills trying to get them out of or off of our race belts. And we have also seen electrolyte pills dissolve in pockets hooked to race belts because they have gotten wet with sweat. One solution to this is to carry the pills in clear plastic baggies and to pin them and the gels to the belts or stuff them in pockets (of the belt or racing suit), or put them in small cylindrical vials that can be shoved under the bottom of your shorts or in a small pocket on your uniform. You just need to remember to grab all this stuff and not leave any of it sitting in a running shoe!

Also, be careful that your race number is secured tightly to your race belt or you risk being penalized for not having your race number showing in front or you as you cross the finish line.

Lost Bib

I once got a two-minute penalty because my race number became soggy and separated from my race belt, unknowingly falling to the ground. The photographers at the finish line could not tell who I was – my body markings had faded too – and that kind of thing upsets them and the race director, who like to make money off finisher photos. Ever since, I use extra safety pins to secure my number to the belt. P.B.

Missing Race Belt

Transitions are a part of the race that is often not practiced enough, meaning that many people lose some time that could be a lot easier to gain than on the swim, bike, or run. I typically pride myself on relatively quick transitions and try to be as quick and efficient as possible. So, as I was finishing my cycling leg at an age-group national championships, I was visualizing how I would quickly go through T2, or the bike-to-run transition. However, things were thrown for a loop when I racked my bike and noticed that my shoes were knocked over. That wasn't a big deal, but I also saw that my race belt with my number was gone! I spent about a minute looking all around the surrounding racks for it to no avail. I finally figured I'd have to take the 2-minute penalty and not waste any more time with the search. As luck would have it, though, right before the run exit of the transition I saw a belt off to the side of the sign. I decided to go over and check just in case and, lo-and-behold, it WAS my race belt. Obviously, someone must have accidentally grabbed it and realized it on their way out of T2 and, rather than putting it back, just tossed it to the side! It was annoying to lose that much time, but I also felt energized by my good luck. D.W.

Tip Nine: Remember that the penalty for a missing race number is typically one or two minutes for sprint or Olympic distance races. If you forget it and it'll cost you more than that to run back and get it, it's not worth it. In that case, risk getting the penalty and cut your losses!

Slippery Suit

The only penalty that I've ever received was a costly one. I had a great race against some very strong competition in Virginia, crossing the line in second overall. It was great because my mother-in-law and uncle had made the trip to watch with my wife in what turned out to be one of my better days to that point in my early triathlon career. However, when the results came out, they had me listed as fourth. I went to find out why, and they said it was because my race number wasn't showing when I crossed the finish line. I did remember seeing my number, because I had worn a new suit and the number kept sliding toward my side as I ran. It never got further than my side, though, because then I'd rub it with my arm and move it back in front. Frustrated, I tried to argue my point to the race official, but to no avail. Maybe it was good in the long run, though, because to this day, well over a decade later, I think of that every time I get close to the finish line during a race and make sure my number is front and center! D.W.

Limb for Limb

One of my favorite stories took place several years ago at Ironman Lake Placid. Monette and her sister, Katie, decided that they wanted to do an Ironman and settled on Lake Placid. Meanwhile, Katie had a good friend who was one of the top amputee athletes who had stopped doing triathlons to focus on other sports. But, when he found out Katie was doing the race he made up his mind to come out and race again. Obviously, being an amputee, he had some special circumstances that he had to consider, such as putting on a leg for the long run from the water to the transition area and changing legs for the bike and run.

I was spectating with friends and family and we all decided to hang out at a bar up on the main street up the road. We were having a good time and then something caught our attention, luckily. They had live local coverage of the race and the bar was actually showing it on their T.V. What caught our attention was that they mentioned our friend saying that he "was flying on the course and approaching the bike to run transition with a chance to break the Ironman record for amputee athletes". Meanwhile, his then girlfriend, who is his wife now, was at the bar with us ... with his running leg! She gasped, grabbed the leg, and ran out of there as fast as she could. The rest of us had a good laugh as we followed him into T2 on the television and we saw her running to get there just in time to help him change his legs, none the wiser to how close she was to not being there. He did go on to break the record and all was good, but that was one close call and lucky series of events. D.W.

Applying the PREPARE Approach

In negotiating T2, it pays to **PREPARE**. Develop a **Plan** for how you will deal with your bike shoes, dismount your bike, run through transition, find your transition spot, rack your bike, unhook your helmet, put on your running shoes, change any other clothing, put on sunscreen, and gather all the stuff you want to take with you on the run.

Rehearse exactly how you will remove your bike shoes and dismount – many times – and don't try anything new on race day. Also practice how you will wheel your bike to the transition spot and how you will put on your running shoes and gather your race belt, hat, food, pills, or other things. Make sure that you have set things up to minimize the chances that you will leave anything behind, such as in a bag or shoes, and be sure that you have a system that minimizes the chances of dropping your food or pills as you take off.

Try hard to **Execute** your T2 plan and don't get caught up with trying to win the prize for fastest T2, since forgetting to take nutrition with you or to wear your race number, sunscreen, or a hat can cost you much more time in bonking or penalties than you can gain by flying through transition. If surprises emerge in T2, such as confronting a mudhole in your path or finding another bike racked where your bike is supposed to be racked, don't panic, just **Persist** and roll with the punches, quickly finding an alternative way to deal with the situation. Thinking about these possible obstacles before the race, and about what you might do to get around them, is a good idea.

If something goes wrong during T2, take some time after the race to **Analyze** why this happened. Was it something outside of your control (e.g., weather, unseen potholes, reckless competitors)? Were you just simply forgetful (e.g., leaving items in your running shoes) or did you overlook the need to run through a checklist before a race? **Revise** your plan for the next race and start practicing dismounts, bike racking, shoe changes, and so forth.

Finally, try to **Enjoy** T2. Having the swim and the bike behind you can provide a feeling of exhilaration (or maybe relief), and you can feel good about being back on solid earth again. As we said with T1, wave to the fans and have a smile on your face, and that will help you take off on the run with an extra burst of energy.

7 – RUNNING

You're tired, you've already swum and cycled hard. Your body has to adjust from being in a supine and then seated position to running where there is a lot more movement and pressure on your organs and intestines within seconds. The day is getting hotter and the humidity has been taking its toll on your body. Think things can sometimes not go the way you expect? You bet! The more you know what can go wrong and what signals to look out for the better off you'll be. Of course, we hope that you can learn something from some of our experiences that we'll share in this chapter.

Sensitive Feet

I broke the cardinal rule in my second ever Ironman race. My training had gone really well and I couldn't wait to see what I could do. I had never been faster in running and made a game-day decision that it could make me run a couple of minutes faster if I wore my lighter racing flats instead of the shoes I had been planning on wearing. I'd worn them to do my speed work in, so they should be fine, right? Um, no. I did have a great race, although the run became very painful about halfway through. I'm sure I lost several minutes, even though I still had a good finishing time, because I wound up breaking the bones on the outsides of both feet during the run! I couldn't even attempt to really walk for several days afterwards! My wife, Monette, got me on video saying that I would never do another Ironman shortly after finishing. Of course, the next day I found out that I had qualified for Kona and eagerly signed up without hesitation. D.W.

Few things are worse than trying to run as you start to chafe, your feet start to blister, your nipples begin bleeding, or any of the other unfortunate issues that can arise while running in a triathlon. Having a successful day can be as simple as being sure to have enough lubricant, such as Body Glide or Chamois Butt'r for your feet, nipples, groin, underarms, etc.

Sudsy Shorts

Perhaps the most commonly broken "rule" in triathlon is to never try something new on race day. You never know what can happen if you haven't tried it before; sometimes it can work, cause pain, or just be really funny. A few years back, Monette had an experience that was mostly in the funny category during a half iron distance triathlon.

Monette really needed a good pair of shorts to race in, but didn't have time to buy them until the days just prior to the triathlon. However, she finally managed to find some that she was excited to wear. It's just a pair of shorts. What can possibly go wrong, right? Well, something quite unexpected happened.

As soon as Monette started to come down a hill during the run where I was with some friends cheering her on, we were wondering what was all over her shorts. Then, as she got closer, we were all laughing because her shorts were covered in SUDS. Yes, that's right, her shorts were literally sudsing up as she was racing. We happened to be near an aid station and yelled to her what was going on and she said that it had been happening the whole race. She decided to try to wash it down with some water from the table. Of course, that just made it worse! She spent the rest of the race, in which she did really well by the way, trying to keep the suds at bay as best she could. On the other hand, because she kept dumping water on her legs, she ended up with bloody and blistered feet from running in sopping wet shoes. Our theory

afterwards was that the shorts may have been returned by someone who had washed them without using the spin cycle. That was the only thing we could think of that would cause shorts to suds uncontrollably. This did earn Monette the nickname 'Suds' for a while. D.W.

Tip One: Wear clothing that is tested and you can run comfortably in!

That's a Good Look

While we recommend not trying anything new on race day, you sometimes have no other choice. Monette's sister showed up for a marathon before realizing that she had forgotten her socks. With no time to buy a new pair her only option was to wear her black knee-high business socks. I guess it didn't slow her down too much, though, as she went on to qualify for the Boston Marathon. I'm sure people were wondering what new method or type of compression she was trying! D.W.

Doctoring Yourself

One of our friends is an Orthopedic Surgeon and a top-level triathlete. We were entered in the World Duathlon Championships in Spain a few years ago in a race that was a 10K run, followed by a 40K bike and then a 5K run. The first 10K run involved four 2.5K loops, a major portion of which had an out-and-back route, and this allowed you to see the people in front of you four times if you were basically keeping up with them. Our friend had a bit of a lead on me, but I was able to wave to him on each of the first three loops. However, on the fourth loop, I didn't see him, and I figured he had just gotten so far ahead of me that he had passed the out-and-back portion before I got there. I was in such a zone that I didn't notice that there were medical personnel tending to a competitor as I passed through that portion.

It turns out that the injured competitor was my friend – and his tibia had broken while running, reportedly with a deafening and sickening crack! Apparently, he knew he had a stress fracture in that leg, having X-rayed it himself right before the trip, but he thought he could make it through the World Championships and then rest it. He made the classic doctor's medical error of serving as his own doctor, and he paid the price of having to be rushed to a local hospital and then enduring a painful flight home. Fortunately, everything turned out fine and he is back competing again at a high level. P.B.

Pushing Too Much

I'll never forget my first running race. I was twelve years old and entered a local 10k with a few good friends from my swim team. We ran every once in a while as training for swimming, but never any real distance. But, like most young athletes, I had to learn about pacing the hard way. I took it out hard, full of adrenaline, youthful exuberance, and the love of speed. I held the leader in my sights until after two miles. Then, predictably, I spent several minutes stopped and throwing up along the side of the road. I struggled through the rest of the race, humbled and sore. We later learned that the winner was a local runner using it as a training race for the Olympic trials. Looking back, I should have probably been thrilled that I held that close to him for as long as I did. But, that thought didn't enter my twelve-year-old brain! Actually, I guess I didn't learn my lesson as much as I should have as I became notorious for pushing myself to the point of puking after every triathlon I did for many years until I was well into my twenties, some of which were quite spectacular messes. D.W.

Tip Two: Pushing yourself is good. Pushing yourself too far is not. Learn to tell the difference!

When you hit the run portion of a triathlon, plenty of things can still go wrong. Indeed, problems during the run are extremely common, especially because many people push themselves way too hard on the swim and bike, leaving no energy – and sometimes little mental acuity – for the run. Problems can surface with:

· Staying on Course

- Avoiding Cramps and Bonking

- Avoiding Injuries and Health Problems

Stories and advice for dealing with these issues follow.

Staying on Course

Misguided

Being a coach, you try to give your athletes as much guidance as you can to prepare them for all kinds of different contingencies. Then, when you're on the course waiting for an athlete to come in, and keep waiting, and waiting, ... it can get nerve-racking. This has happened way to often, especially with the collegiate team that I coach.

On one particular occasion, I was waiting nervously for one of my athletes to come in during our collegiate conference championships, where she had been having a great race with a real potential to finish in the top three after an incredible ride. Seeing the pace that the first one to finish held and not seeing second yet, I felt encouraged that second may even be possible. However, second came in and, then, third a bit later, with no UNC jersey (my team) in sight. What happened? Finally, she came in fourth place, but with a much slower run than she should have had.

What happened was that she took a wrong turn and it took a good amount of time to realize it! She had been running well and gotten to a point where she couldn't see anyone and was led off course by a volunteer. Without having people around and being on a curvy path, it was a while before she realized that she must be off course and had to retrace her steps. She still managed an amazing race and wouldn't make that mistake again. Oops, scratch that. The very next year at the conference championships she was again led off course, this time during the bike! This time she rode an additional several miles before realizing it and turning around. When she got back to the intersection and asked the cop there why he didn't direct her where to go, he simply said: "I didn't think you were part of the race"! This one cost her a lot more time, but she took the pressure of a top finish off of her chest and enjoyed the day and team camaraderie. D.W.

Too Eager to Finish

Aquathlon is another sport in which we compete. In warm weather, the distances are typically 2.5K run, 1000 meter swim, 2.5K run. When the water is cold and wetsuits are allowed – when the water temperature is under 72 degrees in international races and 78 degrees in U.S. races – it is recognized that putting on a wetsuit after a first run would be unworkable, so these races are changed to a 1000 meter swim and a 5K run. This swim-run format was what Shelly was doing at the World Aquathlon Championships in London in September, 2013.

She had an excellent swim and was among the leaders in her age group, as she went off on the 5K run. The run course had two loops around Hyde Park, with competitors going straight past the swim start/finish area at the end of the first loop. At the end of the second loop, they did a U-turn right before the swim start/finish to enter a 250 meter finishing chute to dash for the finish line.

I was cheering Shelly on from near the swim start/finish and she looked great coming in from her first loop, still among the leaders. But then she inexplicably did the U-turn into the finishing chute, a lap sooner than she should have. I screamed at her to turn around, but she couldn't hear me. Fortunately, the race announcer was on the job and stated over the loudspeaker: "Here comes Shelly Bloom, our first finisher in the women's 60 to 64 age group, with an incredible time!" Hearing this about 100 meters from the finish line, Shelly yelled out "Oh Shit!" and realized her mistake. She turned around, entered the run course back where she made her wrong turn, which the rules allow, and did the second lap and the U-turn again – finishing fifth, the same place she was when she had her goof-up. We estimate that she lost only about 45 seconds with this mistake, as the adrenaline rush she got after the mistake probably made up some time. P.B.

Tip Three: Bike or run the run course beforehand if possible, or at least know what the directional signs or markers look like. Stay on course!

Staying on course should be much easier to do during the run than it is during the swim and bike. Obviously, when running, you have less trouble seeing where you're going because you are traveling at a slower rate of speed. Nevertheless, distractions, fatigue, poor signage, following the wrong competitors, or inattentive volunteers can lead to you making a wrong turn. In a tired, sweaty state, you can miss the sign that tells you where to turn or the shout from a volunteer that tells you that you're going the wrong way. Problems can especially arise in multiple loop courses, where people lose count or get confused about which way they should go.

Scouting the run course in advance can help avoid these problems. Study the signs and road markers, and pay particular attention to what the terrain is like right before a turn or chute, so that you can recognize the turns quickly and plow right through them. As mentioned with the bike ride, if you hit a point of uncertainty about directions, don't hesitate being vocal and yelling to other competitors or volunteers, asking "Which way?"

Avoiding Cramps, Bonking, and Complete Burn Out

Heat Exhaustion

Throughout the years I have had several severe issues racing in the heat. Not surprisingly, each one came with it's own twist and lesson learned. The first instance occurred when I was in college and my dad and roommate came up to Maryland to watch me race on what was one of the first hot days of the year. During school, I was on the swim team through the spring and it had been pretty chilly after that, so I didn't have much of an opportunity to acclimate to the heat. Hindsight being 20/20, I had all of the classic symptoms of heat illness, but didn't realize it at the time. I vividly remember that I stopped sweating, started to get chill bumps, then got tunnel vision and became disoriented. For better or worse, there was another competitor that saw that I was struggling and helped keep me going, literally pushing me with his hand on my back to get me up a hill. After I finished, I collapsed and was out for a little while. When I started to come to, I was in a tub of ice and people were pouring bags of ice directly on top of me. It took a long time for my senses to come back and days before I started to feel normal again. Meanwhile, my mom and dad tried to convince me that it might be time to retire! D.W.

Delirious Running

Not only can the air get hot and muggy in South Carolina, but the water can get downright soupy. At one particular race that I did, the air temperature was in the 80s but, even worse, the water temperature was around 90 degrees. The reason I had signed up for the race was as a tune up for nationals and try everything out that I would race in a few weeks later. This included a new black speed suit. Note, while these suits may make you swim a bit faster, they are not optimal in hot water! Half way through the swim, I started to get really hot and had the familiar tunnel vision issue. I did slow down and was able to manage the damage a bit for a while. However, the second issue hit me on the bike. I drank a lot early on because of the swim, but there wasn't an aid station and I ran out of liquid with about five miles left on the bike course. Saying that I got thirsty is an understatement. Even with that, I managed to come off of the bike in the lead and started off the run pretty well. However, I faded steadily throughout the run and was passed somewhere on the course. The interesting part came at the end of the run. I was running down a little hill with two quick turns toward the finish line, which was within sight. By this point I was getting pretty delirious and was a bit out of it. Monette was standing at the corner where I was to turn left followed by a quick right, and this segment was patrolled by a policeman with his car parked at the corner. My mind saw the turn, but my body just didn't want to cooperate and I ended up running (okay, more like shuffling) right into the police car! Monette asked if I was okay and if I could make it to the finish line just down a short hill. Somehow, I kept going, passed the line, and immediately proceeded to collapse. Another pool of cold water and ice was in my near future along with an extended recovery! D.W.

Beaten by the Heat

I knew when it was announced that age group Olympic distance nationals were scheduled to be in Tuscaloosa, AL in August that it was likely to be hot. Unfortunately, that didn't stop me from making the mistakes leading me toward another heat-related episode. I wore my speed suit again in warm water with a strong current. Because of the current, the swim took a lot longer than normal with much more energy than usual. However, this was good for me coming from a swimming background. I came out with the leaders and was really pumped, although already hot. Since I was out front, I started the bike hard right away and was flying on the fun course. It wasn't until the last few miles that I realized that I was literally cooking and starting to suffer. By this point in my career, I knew it was bad when I stopped sweating and got chill bumps. But, my ego got the best of me yet again as I was still doing really well. By the first mile of the run, though, I had nothing left and severe tunnel vision. I literally could only see a sliver of what was in front of me. For some reason, I felt it more important to still finish the race rather than drop out of a triathlon for the first time. I did manage to finish the race again, walking/ shuffling much of the way in a delirious haze. Crossing the finish line I passed out cold and fell face-first into the grass. When I came to, a poor young nurse had me on my side and was taking my core temperature - yes, rectally! This time I was in really bad shape and had to go back in after collapsing again when eventually released the first time. I was cramping so bad that I was basically spasming randomly while trying to lie down. IV's, ice, cold towels, liquids, etc. were how I spent much of the rest of my day after the race. Looking back, it is obvious that I could have caused some serious damage and would have been much better off dropping out! D.W.

Ambulance Ride

It was quite an interesting experience at the Washington Olympic distance triathlon that I used as prep during Ironman training. This was my first time down there and the venue was fantastic, with some good fast competition toeing the line. The morning was beautiful, if a little muggy, and the water was 83 degrees. Just a little hot, but not too bad.

I felt really good on the swim, probably the best that I've felt in a race in quite some time. Coming out of the water and into transition, I realized that I had a big lead, as no one was in transition yet by the time I was on the road and around the corner on my bike.

There was a pretty decent headwind for much of the beginning of the ride, but I kept it steady and strong. I never felt great, but pretty good, and enjoyed the course. I drank a full bottle of Infinit and about half a bottle of water, which is about right for an hour ride and 26 miles. I bring that up because of what happened later. Of course, I had no idea what was going on behind me but had been riding pretty strong and figured I likely didn't lose much time, if any.

Starting the run, I still didn't feel great but not that terrible either. I did joke to a fellow competitor that was on course doing the sprint distance (going on simultaneously) that I would pay her to run the two laps for me if I could run the one lap for her, but she wouldn't take me up on it. The course is a two loop out-and-back, so on the way back in I saw that I had a big lead of at least a mile and was really pumped about that. On the way in toward the end of the first loop my legs started to really get oddly fatigued and I slowed considerably. But having such a big lead, I was fine just backing off and cruising it in. The next mile and a half didn't feel good, but still not absolutely horrible. However, after making the last turn toward home I started to feel really off. I thought it was just excessive fatigue, but the distance and pace shouldn't have been a problem at all so I should have realized it was more than that. Someone told me later it was in the 80s maybe, but also 90% humidity, which certainly contributed.

Then, it hit me fast. With about a half mile left, going over a bridge, I went down. I remember grabbing the guard rail, but not much after that for a while. I found out afterward that a friend saw me go down and I asked her to get help, which she gratefully did. Thank you, Paula! It's weird to not remember much. I have vague memories of some people stopping and I told them to go on and to not call 911. I've since found out some embarrassing things that I said or did, such as that I kept saying that I was in the lead and wanted to finish, when that was obviously out of the question. Really, the next thing I remember was getting ice dumped and thrown all over me. The race director, Brent Dorenkamp, was incredible and I owe him a huge thank you as well. I do remember throwing up a good amount, but don't remember being put into a truck or the fact that they moved me. The good news, though, is that while that is the case I do now remember answering questions and knew everything except the date, which I wasn't too far off from. However, I did have an issue remembering my social security number later. I know that I owe others for stopping as well, and am very sorry that I don't remember who was there.

It seems like it happened very shortly after I passed out, but the next thing I know emergency crews are asking questions and taking care of me. I remember hearing a couple of other friends helping out. When they tried to move me, I couldn't stand on my legs and they put me on a gurney, although the order of events may have been different than that as I'm not sure who asked or when they tried to get me to stand. As they moved me into the ambulance, I threw up several more times including while in the ambulance, which was not fun at all. However, I did start to feel better and come to at that point. That's why I was a little surprised when they checked me over and the guy told the driver to 'go hot' and the sirens went on as the driver stepped on the gas! They said they had to put me on oxygen and I'm not sure what my blood pressure was, but a good while later while at the hospital it was still only about 100/55, and they had a little trouble getting an IV needle in because I was 'dry' and it took a couple of veins to get right.

In the ER, they were still keeping me on ice and started the IVs while also taking a lot of other tests. It's odd, because by that

point I was starting to feel much better so I was surprised when they came back and told me that they wanted me to stay overnight because my kidney function was way off, while my electrolytes were as well. Other numbers were also off, which I found out later, and which I was told was basically like poisoning my body. They told me more than once that I'm not 21 and have to take added precautions! I know that, and thought that I had, but just didn't have enough liquid/ice on the 10k run.

Also, poor Monette had to get the news via several voicemails after training with a client at home and was very gracious in making the trip down to be with me. I can't tell you how big of a lift it was to have her there.

My functions eventually stabilized back into normal ranges and they allowed me to come home. Afterwards, I just needed a lot of SLEEP! It was scary and embarrassing, but I'll learn from it and move on. D.W.

Tip Four: Know the signs of heat sickness and know when to stop pushing.

As far as gastrointestinal issues, the longer the race, the more competitors you will see suffering with cramps and bonking during the run, often being forced to walk long distances because running has become so painful and difficult. Many will also become nauseous and vomit during the run, or they can end up making emergency pit stops in the porta-potties, woods, or someplace less discreet.

Photogenic

A fun aspect of many races is that they will have photographers at the finish and often along the course as well. Monette and her sister Katie always make a point to look for these photographers during their races to the point that I joke that according to these many photos, I would think that Katie runs with her arms constantly up in the air! Well, we jokingly started to tell our running clinics on our last class before the race that it was important to always look good for the photographers. No matter how you felt, you had to perk up and try to show good form or, at least, some enthusiasm. One of our groups really took us to heart and enjoyed 'posing' every time a camera was pointed their way. One girl in particular had us rolling as her pictures showed her kissing her biceps, exaggerating her running stride, and other various funny poses! On the other opposite side of this, I've had two separate friends who have finisher photos showing them literally tripping and trying to catch themselves as they cross the line. D.W.

And, Not Photogenic

The Memphis in May Triathlon used to be a very big race, and the only Olympic distance triathlon that was an Ironman World Championship qualifier. It's an awesome race and I gave it everything I had on a relatively hot day. As I came into the last 1/4 mile or so, I was having trouble holding the contents of my stomach in. I was determined to get to the finish line first, though. Two hundred meters, one hundred meters, I'm almost there but my cheeks are puffing out and it's starting to come up. Oh no, just as I approach the line, it was impossible to hold it anymore and I projectiled ... right onto a volunteer kneeling down ready to take my timing chip! To make matters worse, they were filming this particular race and had a scaffolding with the camera and an announcer at the finish line and I could hear him say, "oooh, that's not good!". D.W.

The Famous Kona Finish Line

The finish at the Ironman World Championships is arguably the most amazing experience in triathlon, if not sports in general. That is, if you can remember it! I had another client who was in phenomenal shape starting the race a few years back. He had worked on a great game plan and was physically ready for the day, which promised to be one of the hottest and most humid in many years.

The swim went according to plan and he got out onto the bike without issue. Much of the ride went well, too, but he started to fade toward the end of it. Figuring it was just natural fatigue he pressed on and finished the ride. Onto the run, he didn't feel right; sluggish, full, and oddly tired. Having to slow to a walk in places, friends on the course described him as looking 'out of it'. Amazingly, he did finish the race, staggering down Alii Drive and across the line that is the dream of thousands of triathletes across the world. Unfortunately, he doesn't remember any of it. He sat down and started to slur his speech. Then, when his wife came over he didn't even recognize her! Uh oh, that's not good.

They took him to the fantastic medical team on site to look him over. Believe it or not, he had actually GAINED 8 pounds during the race. What happened was that, being such a hot and humid day, he stuck to his plan of fueling, electrolytes, and fluid, but then figured it was a good idea to take in an additional bottle of water per hour. This caused him to dilute his electrolyte balance and go severely hyponatremic and even had some bleeding on his brain. Luckily, they got him to the hospital where he would spend the next day getting treatment and recovering. He wasn't allowed to come home for several days, but being stuck in Kona didn't upset him too much! Fortunately, he did recover fully, knows who his wife is, and is back to competing on an elite level again. That's one I don't want to ever see repeated! D.W.

Tip Five: Stay hydrated and fueled, but also be careful not to eat too much or take in too much solid food. In longer races, such as Ironman races, you also have to be careful to not take in too much water to avoid hyponatremia.

Muscles get sore and fatigued as lactic acid builds up in them. Glycogen is needed for the muscles to function, and for a while your muscles can get plenty of it from your fat stores and from the fluids and food you take in while exercising. The glucose in those fluids and foods becomes glycogen. But at some point when you are pushing yourself beyond your lactate threshold, your body cannot replace muscle glycogen quickly enough, causing lactate to build up. Doing intensity training at above your lactate threshold, generally when you find yourself doing very heavy breathing, along with workouts alternating below and slightly above threshold, can help with lactate tolerance and increase lactate clearance as your body learns how to rid the muscles of lactic acid more efficiently, delaying the point where the your muscles start to get drained. But in longer races, again, such as Ironman events, many will still hit a point where their muscles fatigue no matter how much you have trained or taken in fluids and food, because it's very difficult or unwise to mimic that effort and distance in training except for a select few. This is where experience plays such an important role in triathlons. Learning how your body responds and how to deal with it is the goal of all of those training hours.

Tip Six: Learn what it feels like when you go above your lactate threshold and try to train to sustain a pace as close to that as you can.

Still, the best way to limit cramping and bonking problems is through practicing how you will execute your intake of fluids and nutrition, as well as how you will pace yourself. If you can afford it and fit it into your schedule, this practice can also be done in races that you consider B or C races (not your goal race, but of secondary or tertiary importance), not A ones (your goal race). If your A race is a sprint or Olympic distance, getting in practice efforts with your hydration, nutrition, and pacing plan (after swimming and biking), should be quite feasible.

Tip Seven: Having smaller races to experiment in before your big race, if you have one, can be a big benefit.

However, if your A race is a half ironman or longer, then longer practice sessions may be difficult or even counterproductive, as they may require too much recovery time and take away precious training that could be used to improve. Of course, this depends on your background, what kind of shape you're in, and how your recent training has been going. In this case, it may be better to practice your hydration, nutrition, and pacing plan with a short swim, long bike ride (could be longer than the actual distance), followed by a shorter to moderately long run. Many people overemphasize the doing of a long run after a long bike, but, again, this should be done sparingly, if at all. Doing about 30-minutes after the bike is often enough to get you the feel that you need while leaving you energy to do a better longer run that your body will get more adaptation from. Of course, this is also dependent on the person!

Tip Eight: Practice bricks, where you run off of the bike in training. The more experience you have running off of the bike, the better you'll be able to know what to expect and get up to race speed.

Just like with cycling, you need to learn what your gut can tolerate well in terms of drinks, gels, chews, tablets, and pills that can give you the fuel and electrolytes you need to keep going in the race. However, it's often much more difficult to digest things on the run, as your stomach is sloshing around more than it does during the relative calmness on the bike, especially in a race. Everybody's gut is different, so while there are general guidelines, there is no magic formula that will work for everyone. Trial and error – or even a triathlon nutrition expert – will largely guide you on the fluids and nutrition. In longer races, many people don't take in enough fluids or nutrition, partly because it can sicken them, or they're going harder than they should and can't digest the fuel. One should strive to learn how to avoid that dilemma. At the same time, you don't want to overdrink, especially without taking in enough electrolytes, as that can lead to hyponatremia in longer events lasting several hours. And you don't want to force food in and overeat, as that can cause GI problems or, at the very least, sluggishness.

Do the Dew

After practicing with different fueling options and drinks, Monette came up with a fairly unique game plan for Ironman Lake Placid during one of her races there. Being someone who doesn't drink sodas, she found out that sipping on a Mountain Dew really helped pick her up. The sugars and caffeine had a great effect. So, she put it in her special needs bag during the race and that gave her something to look forward to as she did her run. Besides, the fact that Mountain Dew isn't a very common choice for Ironman race fuel, the next dilemma was where to put the bottle as she really didn't want to carry it in her hands the whole time. So, what she did was put it in her top that she was wearing. We got a kick out of her race pictures as you could see the bottle clearly in many of them. She claims that it worked perfectly and she did have a very good race. D.W.

Fuel on a Stick

A friend was getting toward the end of a marathon, but could tell that she was on the verge of hitting the wall. As she came up to an aid station, she was looking to grab anything to get some quick carbs in. She saw that they had something on a stick. Thinking that this was clever and that it was something similar to gu or honey, she grabbed it and put it in her mouth. Some of you reading this may remember that they used to offer these sticks in some bigger marathons. No, it wasn't any kind of gel, it was Vaseline to put on a spot that may be chafing! Needless to say, she realized her mistake quickly. D.W.

Tip Nine: Learn what nutrition will be offered on the course. If you can practice using what the race will offer, it is nice to not have to carry extra bottle on your bike or a fuel belt during the run.

Finally, don't forget about your running pace. Keeping a steady pace or doing negative splits usually works better for most competitors than going all out at the beginning and burning yourself out. Poor pacing can make for a rough day and frustrating performance, whereas being a little more patient and controlled can make for a fun and strong finish.

Tip Ten: Give your legs a little time to get into a fluid rhythm and good leg extension of running without trying to force it as soon as you get off of the bike.

Avoiding Injuries and Health Problems

Racing When Injured

It's a bad idea to race when you have the type of injury that can be aggravated by pushing yourself the way you tend to do when racing. However, most of us have to learn this the hard way, as our friend the Orthopedic Surgeon did (see the story at the start of this chapter). My worst experience in this regard was with an injury to my shin. It wasn't too serious, but it did keep me from racing for two months.

The injury started while attending a yoga class. While yoga is very good for triathletes, the particular class I went to was led by a couple who tried to get you to stretch every single muscle and tendon the way they showed you. Unfortunately, I'm not very flexible and in trying to point my toes a certain way, I felt something pop on the front of my lower leg. But it was only a little sore afterwards and I ignored it. I continued to swim, bike, and run, and I even took a trip to London where I did a ton of walking. All that walking seemed to aggravate the soreness, yet I still thought it would go away. I didn't hesitate to enter a race the week after I returned from London, and my swim and bike went well. However, during the run my shin became really sore, and after the race it blew up like a balloon. There was a stress reaction there that needed rest, ice, anti-inflammatories, and more rest. After two months, it was totally better and it has never bothered me again. But I don't go to those yoga classes anymore – and I don't race when something really hurts! P.B.

Tip Eleven: Know what is a 'good pain' and what constitutes a 'bad pain' and can lead to worse injuries.

The best advice we can give here is "Know your body!" Recognize when muscles, tendons, or bones are damaged enough before a race that it is wiser for you to decline to do the race or enter a different kind of race at the same venue that doesn't present a risk to your injured body part. Some races have an Aquabike option (swim-bike), which is good for people with foot or knee problems, and other races have a Duathlon option (run-bike-run), which is good for people with shoulder problems. If something snaps or seizes up during the run, don't be embarrassed to drop out and save yourself for another day. And if you are overheating badly because of hot weather conditions, a lack of ice at aid stations, or poor pre-race conditioning on your part, calling it a day may be a very wise option.

Change of Pace

I had some lofty goals one season when Monette and I went down to do the Kiawah marathon with a group of friends. Things were going according to plan until mile 16. Between miles 15 and 16 I had fallen ten seconds off of my pace. In case you don't know about Kiawah, saying it is completely flat is an understatement. So, after 16 miles of very uniform strides, I tried to pick it up, and as soon as I did I ripped my groin. It was excruciating and I was forced to stop. I couldn't walk, let alone run. I was near an aid station and they called it in, but it would be a long time for a vehicle to pick me up due to all of the runners. One funny thing that happened was that Monette eventually ran past me looking strong, but was obviously a little confused as she yelled over asking me how I did, thinking that I had already finished and was out spectating. The second memorable event was how I got back to the finish line. Five police officers wearing kilts and playing bagpipes were driving in an open jeep along the course to make sure everything was going okay and entertaining the runners and crowd. When they saw me they kindly asked if I needed a ride.

Not wanting to wait any longer, I gladly accepted. It was quite a sight, though, as I had to squeeze between two rather large bagpipe players in the back seat. To make matters worse, we drove up the finishing straight just as a good friend of mine was finishing in third overall. So, many friends and friends' spouses, girlfriends, kids, etc. were out there cheering him on and had a hearty laugh as they saw me in the jeep. It was a long time before I lived that one down! D.W.

It shouldn't be a surprise, but there is research showing that even by putting something in your mouth that will force you to curve your lips up, you will enhance your mood and performance. No matter how you feel, try to smile at people. In fact, the worse you feel, try to do it more! The more tense you get, the more you focus on how tired you're getting, or the more you get frustrated by other people's actions, the harder or less fun the run will be.

Big Expectations

It's always great when my parents are able to come to a race with me. The first year that I moved down to North Carolina, they came to watch me compete in a local Half Ironman in which I was underprepared and had a rough race. So, it was a pleasure when they came down the following year to see me give it another shot. I had trained pretty well and was excited to show them what I was capable of.

To make a long story short, I stayed strong throughout and had a good day. As I ran down the long straightaway toward the finish in third place overall, I was looking for my parents. There they are! I noticed them right as I was running past them. My mom wasn't looking and my dad was reading a paper! After I finished, I walked over to them and laughed at their surprise. My mom exclaimed, "I told you so!" It turns out that she thought that was me coming, but when she told my dad he checked his watch and said something to the order of, "No, it can't be. He's got at least another half hour or so." They've been to many races since and have become quite the expert spectators, but this still makes me laugh. D.W.

Sometimes, you have to be careful not to get caught up in the excitement of the crowd, aid station, or other situations that can spike your adrenaline and cause you to do something unwise. We're sure you've heard the stories of athletes hurting themselves celebrating, jumping, doing a sudden sprint to the finish, etc. It does happen. When you've been doing one motion for a long time your muscles don't like sudden changes.

Tip Twelve: Smile, thank volunteers, and keep a calm demeanor.

Triathletes Can't Jump

Ironman Austria is a fantastic race and a lot of fun. At one spot in town that you hit twice during the run there is a bell that you are encouraged to jump up and ring. With all of the excitement and fun spectators, I gladly jumped and rang the bell on the first lap. On the second lap, I was starting to feel the miles fatiguing my legs, but I wanted to get that cheer and hear the crowd. So, I came up to the bell, jumped up, and failed miserably to jump high enough to ring it! It wasn't very high, but my vertical jump of a couple of inches obviously wasn't going to cut it. D.W.

Applying the PREPARE Approach

It is essential to **PREPARE** for the run. You need a **Plan** for how you will hydrate, eat, and pace yourself. Where and what will you drink? Will you do it only at aid stations or will you carry liquids with you? Will you consume sports drinks or just plain water? Where and what will you eat? Will you eat at certain mileage markers or at the aid stations on the course? Will you carry foods in pockets or on your race belt? Will you try to maintain a steady pace or will you go out fast and see if you can hold on? The distance of the race will have a big influence on how you answer these questions, with longer races requiring more planning and deliberating.

As stressed, it is essential to **Rehearse** how you will hydrate and consume food. Learn what works well with your gut and what tends to create problems. Practice holding a certain pace for long intervals. Get your body used to the strain it will undergo during the run and it will be less likely to rebel with cramps or injuries.

Execute your plan and drink, eat, and pace the way you intended to the best of your ability. This is especially important if the race is long and if the temperature is hot. If you spill a drink or drop a gel, don't panic, but **Persist** and try to replace what you missed with products available at the next aid station. As a general rule, you shouldn't take food or drinks from fans or strangers along the route, but if you dropped something you might have to replace it with one of these offerings.

If you end up cramping, bonking, or getting sick, do your best to **Analyze** what caused it. Were the temperatures just too hot compared to the conditions in which you trained? Would you have been better off if you had put more ice in your cap, down your shorts, and on your wrists? Did the flavor of your drinks or gels, or the amount of caffeine they had in it, seem to upset your stomach? **Revise** your plan for the next race and start practicing how you will do things differently.

More than anything, **Enjoy** the run and, even if you're not feeling the greatest, try hard to ignore your discomfort and be happy that the race is almost over. Think about how much fun you will have recounting your race story to your friends and family in the coming days. Thank the volunteers and fans along the course and give high-fives to people as you go down the finishing chute (unless it will cost you a place on the podium). Pump your fists in triumph as you cross the finish line, and make sure that you smile at the race photographers at that moment. You won't want to show people a finishing picture of you with a look of anguish on your face!

8 – POST-RACE COOL-DOWN AND RECOVERY

The competitive race may be over when you cross the finish line, but your total race experience doesn't end there. What you do right after a race and even during the ensuing days can impact your health, your finances, and your ability to race successfully in the future.

Total Body Cramping

The Eagleman Half-Ironman on Maryland's Eastern Shore was the scene of my fastest half-ironman ever, so I was eager to go back the next year and see if I could do even better. Unfortunately, I didn't do nearly as well as the previous year, and I experienced a memorable post-race disaster that I hope never to repeat again.

I probably shouldn't have been doing the race in the first place. Two weeks before, I had come down with painful back spasms after driving all day and lifting some heavy suitcases. Indeed, while driving to the Eagleman venue two days before the event, my back continued to give me trouble.

On race day, my back felt tight, yet the conditions were pretty good – not too windy or hot – and I was pumped up to compete. I knew a PR was not in the offing, and I was content to just go for a finisher's medal. I had a relatively uneventful and slow race – a little too much walking on the run because of the tightness – and I finished feeling tired but fine. Knowing I had a long drive ahead of me to make it half way back to our summer home in Massachusetts that evening, I gathered up my stuff almost immediately and started walking my bike back to the Bed and Breakfast where I had stayed, about a mile away. I was walking pretty slowly, so I decided to speed things up by riding my bike back to the B&B. Well, as soon as I lifted my leg up to put it over the bike seat, the leg seized up in a cramp that almost knocked me over. So with my now very sore leg – and back – I continued to walk even slower back to the B&B.

When I finally got to the B&B, I realized I had to carry my bike and backpack up about 5 steps to get up to the porch and entrance, where I could leave them and then go in to shower and change. As I climbed the first step, the cramp in my leg returned, and it didn't stop there. My whole body seized up in a set of awful cramps and I fell over on top of my bike, writhing in pain. Fortunately, there were other triathletes on the porch who came to help me untangle myself. Miraculously, I suffered no major injury from the fall and, after an hour of drinking a lot and replenishing my electrolytes, I was able to get up, shower, and head for the road. My bike wasn't so lucky, as the fall broke off one of the crank arms, and that was expensive to replace.

The lesson here is to take the time to cool down after a race. I should have been drinking a lot, dunking my body in the cool water, eating some protein, and stretching a bit, letting my muscles calm down and relax. My impatience with getting on my way cost me a lot of money, and it almost cost me a concussion or other serious injury. P.B.

Tip One: Don't rush right out of the race venue unless you absolutely have to. Refuel, rehydrate, and loosen up!

You want to be attentive to how you deal with:

· Treating immediate post-race ailments and injuries

·   Leaving the venue

·   Restoring your body

Of course, we have some stories and thoughts to share about these matters.

Treating Immediate Post-Race Ailments and Injuries

Blacking Out

We were doing an Olympic distance triathlon at White Lake, North Carolina during the late summer, and it was pretty hot (high 80s). I didn't have a great race, though I felt OK about it since I passed a lot of people that I normally can't match during the 10K run in the blazing hot sun. After I finished, I grabbed a drink and went back to the finish line to watch Shelly come in. Her swim wave had gone off a few minutes after mine, and I saw her burning it up on the out-and-back run course, so I knew she would be right behind me. Sure enough, she showed up almost immediately, with a total finishing time much faster than mine. She really had an outstanding performance, winning her age group by several minutes.

What happened next was very disconcerting. Shelly was exhausted from her effort and immediately sat down on a chair to catch her breath and let her heart rate come down. It took me a little while to realize that Shelly had actually passed out while sitting up in that chair, and it took some time to rouse her and get her to recognize where she was. I tried to get her to drink something and one of the medical people tried to get her to go to the medical tent, but all she wanted to do was dunk herself in the lake, saying it was the most efficient way to cool down. That didn't seem like a bad idea, so I supported her while she walked over to the beach, trying to make sense of some of the unintelligible things she was saying to me. She was really out of it!

When we got to the lake, Shelly waded in and laid down on her back in the shallow water. I quickly recognized that this was terribly dangerous, as she risked becoming submerged if she lost consciousness again. I urged her to stand up, but when she did she promptly buckled. After this scare, it was a lot easier to persuade her to go to the medical tent, where they put in an IV drip of saline solution. It was amazing to see her come to life while hooked to the bag. She was incredibly dehydrated! Later, she admitted that she didn't drink anything on the run. P.B.

After you cross the finish line, it is imperative that you be conscientious about taking care of your body before you leave the race venue. Cool yourself down with ice and/or a dip in the water if you are overheated. Warm yourself up with jackets or blankets and duck into a warm building if you are shivering cold. Replenish your fluids and electrolytes with beverages and try to get some protein to start to allow muscles to repair themselves. Chocolate milk is a great option for getting carbs and protein, and try to get some salt into your body. Some light stretching makes sense, and a bit of massage can help too. Make sure any cramping or stomach problems have subsided before you try to walk or ride somewhere.

Tip Two: Don't just sit or lay down after finishing if you can help it. It usually helps to walk around a little bit first.

If you think something is not quite right after the finish, don't hesitate seeking medical attention! Get ice on that swollen knee, ankle, foot, or pulled muscle; get ointments for scrapes or road rash; get an IV or lots of fluids if you are severely dehydrated. If a friend or family member who knows you well urges you to go to the medical tent, remember that you might not be thinking clearly at that moment and follow their advice. Not to be overly dramatic about it, but taking care of medical issues as soon as possible will save you recovery time and maybe even save your life!

Leaving the Venue

Parking Lot Mudhole

The first time my wife Shelly and I ever qualified for the USA Triathlon Age Group National Championships, it was scheduled to be an Olympic distance event in Kansas City, Missouri. (Note: They have since added a sprint distance National Championship.) We went out there with a bunch of friends and we were having a great time seeing the area, eating together, and going over our race plans.

Race day arrived and we all went out to the transition area and set up our stuff. It was a very nice venue and it added to our excitement. But a few minutes before the first wave was supposed to go off in the swim, violent thunderstorms descended on us and wouldn't quit. The weather forecasts indicated that the storms would continue into the afternoon, making it impossible to just postpone the race for later in the day – the roads and police were only reserved and available for a few hours. They ended up canceling the race out of fear of lightning and slick, dangerous roads, holding a fun-run in the rain as a "substitute." We were all disappointed, although the pain was mitigated by an announcement that everyone who showed up that day would automatically be allowed to enter the Age-Group Olympic Distance World Championships in Hawaii that were going to be held a few months later.

Soaked to the bone and shivering, even though it was summer, we trudged back to our rental car with all our stuff and were looking forward to a hot shower. We got all our wet clothes and our bikes into the SUV and started the motor and turned on the heater. And then we went nowhere for an hour and a half! All the rain had created a huge mudhole in the parking area, and car after car was getting stuck in the mud. We were all getting our exercise for the day trying to push the cars out of the ruts. We had a four-wheel drive vehicle, but that didn't do us any good because we were completely hemmed in by other stuck vehicles. With a lot of pushing and the help of some tow-trucks that someone wisely

called, things finally opened up enough for us to get out of there. We were more exhausted than we would have been had we done the race.

The next year, when Nationals were in Kansas City again, things were dry and it was a great race and venue. Nevertheless, we made sure to park our rental car in a paved parking lot! P.B.

Tip Three: Park according to your post-race plans and not necessarily the first open spot or the closest to the venue.

Sisterly Love

I, too, made the trek with my wife out to the ill-fated Kansas City national championship race that was canceled. Paul has mentioned how crazy it was with the rain, delays, and the mud-bath that the parking lot turned into afterwards, so I won't repeat that aspect of the story from my end. However, the funny thing (in retrospect, that is) that happened to us was that Monette's sister Katie had shown up to surprise us that morning. This was before we had a cell phone and since it was pouring cats and dogs, we decided that we'd be happier sitting in the car and occasionally rolling down the windows to try to hear any announcements. It was obvious that nothing was going to happen anytime soon. I don't remember how long it was, but it was quite a while before they finally announced that they were going to have to cancel the race, but would have a 10k run that participants had the option of doing. So, we finally walked over to the transition area to find Katie standing patiently outside of the transition area where our bikes were, dripping wet and shivering waiting to surprise us! Having no way to get ahold of us and not knowing where we had parked, she looked for our bikes in transition and just waited for us to show up. Monette and I felt so bad that we never went over there race morning to rescue her from getting drenched. We skipped the 10k run and eventually had a very fun and memorable weekend, after finally getting out of the parking lot. D.W.

While it is natural to want to pay more attention in your pre-race planning to how you will race, spending a few moments thinking about a plan for departing from the race venue can save a lot of time and headaches. Remember, you will be tired after the race and not eager to spend time in a traffic jam or to take a long walk back to your car or hotel. Think about where you want to park, what routes you want to take back to your car or hotel, and how much help you might need carrying things. Be mindful of your need to unwind after a race and don't plan to make too fast an exit. Also, in planning your parking and your exit, consider whether you will want to stick around for any award ceremony that will take place. Oftentimes, if you park close to the venue, you won't be allowed to leave until the race is completed. If you can, though, staying for the award ceremony is a nice thing to do whether you win something or not. The triathlete community is incredibly supportive of one another, and it's fun to applaud your fellow triathletes for a job well done!

Delayed and Expensive Travel

There are so many stories that I could tell regarding traveling to and from races. From jet lag, lost luggage, delayed and missing flights, smelly neighbors, car troubles, etc., and I've recounted several of these already... However, there are four such instances that I'll narrow it down to that I hope will entertain you and give you something to think about.

It sometimes really pays to be a little flexible with your travel. On our way home from the World Championships in Hamburg, Germany, we were informed at the airport that they overbooked our flight. The airline had a nice proposal, though. If we were willing to have one additional stop, but only get back home about ten minutes later, they would give us mile credits and a decent amount of cash! That was a no-brainer for us. The money was enough that it paid for our flights and it didn't even cost us any real added time!

The people at the airport on the way home from from China were not as nice, though. The price to travel with a bike has gone up *dramatically over the past decade and is already ridiculously expensive. However, they took the cake. They initially tried to tell us that it was going to be $500 each just for our bike boxes to travel home! Of course, this caused an uproar, but they still only reduced it down to $400. At that point, there's nothing you can really do but pay it. I did write the airline and got a little credit for the issue, but it was anything but pleasant.*

But, I don't know if I've ever felt so badly as I did about our travel home from the World Championships in the Madiera Islands. My parents were in the room next to my wife and I and we were both using what we later learned was an outdated itinerary when the travel agent called asking where we were, "everyone's on the bus waiting for you"! Our itinerary didn't have us leaving for several hours and his call had woken us up that morning. To make matters worse, Monette and I hadn't even packed yet! We flew around stuffing things in suitcases and running as fast as we could. It would have been a close call at the airport, but luckily the flight was a little delayed and we made it okay. But, I could feel everybody's eyes on me the entire time and I was embarrassed and horrified at my mistake. It still gives me a sinking feeling in the pit of my stomach thinking about it.

Finally, this could be some people's worst nightmare. A former client had a fabulous Ironman race finishing in the top ten overall. It was the next day when things didn't go as planned. Her rental car broke down on the way to the awards ceremony. By the time she found a way to the ceremony she had missed the Kona slot call for her age group. She pleaded her case to no avail. It's hard to believe you can have that good of a race, put that much work into something, and then have it ruined by a car breaking down! D.W.

Restoring Your Body

Watch Your Step

I had just done a half-ironman the previous weekend and I had done absolutely nothing athletic in the interim. It was a difficult race in hot conditions and I just didn't feel like doing anything that involved using my sore and tight muscles in the ensuing days. I didn't stretch, swim, ride a bike, spin, get a sports massage, or even do very much walking. Shelly, who hadn't raced the previous weekend, was going out for a run on a paved bike path near a beach, and was then going to do some swimming. So I decided it was time to get off my butt and join her. It was a beautiful day!

Well, I didn't do any warm-up and I was still incredibly tight. Not surprisingly, I couldn't really keep up with Shelly. Hence, with my eyes focused on her instead of the path, I planted my right foot in a little dip in the path that I didn't see in advance. I then heard something snap, while rolling over my ankle in a painful way, and dove into the grass on the side of the bike path, screaming to Shelly to come help me.

X-rays later determined that I had broken the fifth metatarsal on the outside of my right foot. I had to spend numerous uncomfortable hours with my foot in a bucket filled with ice – to reduce the swelling – and I could do no running at all for 10 weeks. I was restricted to some biking and spinning, some pool running, and some swimming (with no pushing off with my right foot). I managed to recover enough to compete (slowly) in the World Championships at the 12-week mark, although my foot still hurt and did so for a while afterwards. The one good outcome of this was that all the ice baths – and probably the rest – somehow cured a case of Achilles tendonitis on the same foot that had plagued me for years. That problem has never returned. P.B.

Tip Four: A little time to rest and recover after a big race will usually do more for your long-term improvement than trying to get right back into the swing of things.

Everyone is different in his/her ability to recover from races and hard workouts. Some of this ability depends on your age – recovery takes longer when you're older – and some of this depends on how fit you were going into the race, how long and difficult the race was, and how you dealt with things immediately after the race. Take it easy in the first few workouts after a tough race, and save the intensity training and endurance sessions for when your body no longer feels sore or drained. As long as you give your body a chance to recover between races, we have no real problem with racing frequently and going through two or three cycles each season of racing-recovery-build-taper-race. But this approach only makes sense if you find your body can handle it. Some people can only do a few races a year with both comfort and success.

Taking On Too Much

I was a little overambitious when I signed up for Ironman Arizona when it was in April, not realizing that I was going to be too busy to put in much time to train properly. Going into the race, my biggest week was only eight hours. It got really windy on the bike and I thought about cutting my losses, but then I saw a 74 year-old woman pushing through with a smile on her face and I realized that I really didn't have a reason to not be enjoying myself. I wish I could find out who that was and thank her because I still think of that moment whenever things get tough in races or practices. I followed my plan, which was to keep it easy and comfortable the whole way and walked through the aid stations of the run. As it turned out, that was a good plan. I've never felt that good at the finish of an Ironman before or since, and ended up just missing qualifying for Kona by a few minutes! So, of course, I figured that I could put in more time and qualify for Kona if I could get into another race. Hence, I jumped right back into things signing up for a half Ironman and then Ironman Coeur d'Alene within the next eight weeks. Remember, I didn't do that much training before Ironman AZ, so didn't have a huge base and had just done the Ironman. The half Ironman went okay. I was in the lead coming off of the bike, but faded from first to sixth during the second half of the run. Chalking that up to being tired from the training I powered on. Fast forward to Coeur d'Alene, and I again come off the bike in front of my age group or close to it. The first six miles or so go okay, but then I start to fade. My legs just had nothing. It was everything I could do to just keep going forward. I did finish, but it took a lot out of me and my poor Dad once again had to listen to me throwing up in the hotel room afterwards because I had pushed myself so hard.

The result of my poor decisions and not recovering adequately was that it was literally three to four MONTHS before I was able to jog more than five miles without getting so tired and dead-legged that I had to stop. If I wasn't going to listen to my body, I guess it was going to force the issue! D.W.

Applying the PREPARE Approach

All the elements of the **PREPARE** acronym apply to what you do after a race. We have stressed that making a **Plan** for what you are going to do after the race, especially about cool down, nutrition, and travel, is important. Additionally, you should **Rehearse** your post-race routine every time you race, fine-tuning what you do and getting yourself ready for your next post-race experience. **Execute** your post-race plan with as much fidelity as possible, but recognize that many unanticipated things can happen after a race that will require you to **Persist** and be creative in coping with the challenges. Don't be afraid to seek help from medical personnel or others. Of course, you should **Analyze** what caused any post-race problems and **Revise** your future post-race plans based on this analysis. Finally, do your best to **Enjoy** the post-race experience. Congratulate others for a job well done by cheering on later finishers and participating in the award ceremony. Have fun meeting up with your friends and taking pictures, and show your appreciation to the volunteers and race managers for their efforts.

9 – ADDITIONAL BONUS STORIES

We hope you were able to learn a thing or two as you laughed along with us. Believe it or not, it was hard to narrow it down to the experiences that we've shared in this book. We'll leave you with a few more stories that we thought could be useful learning experiences. These stories didn't necessarily fit into one of our chapters, or they may have fit more than one.

Sometimes It's Just Not In The Cards

The following is from my race report following Ironman Florida in 2014:

I woke up this morning bruised, banged up, chaffed, sore, and tired, but also still amazed and thrilled that I was able to finish Ironman Florida! If you read the Ironman Florida race page, they tout the fact that the weather is almost always just about perfect with a fun moderate temperature ocean swim and a fast course. Yeah, someone decided to play games with us this year. Every day around the race was absolutely fantastic, both before and after. However, throughout the week the forecast for Saturday showed temperatures that kept dropping and wind that kept rising, finally showing a low of 41 degrees and 20-30 mph winds with gusts over 40 mph on race day! FUN!

After doing Ironman Maryland, I felt I had left a lot on the course and wanted one more shot at putting together a really fast race that I know I am capable of. So, about three weeks before the race I emailed a travel agency that associated with Ironman and asked if they had any more slots. They told me to call them right away, and they were able to get me in as someone had just backed out. I add this to the story because of what happened when I went to check-in. My race number was 813 but the name on the bib that I wore for the race and everything else was AlvaroJavier Cuenca!! Of course, that caused a lot of confusion at registration and took a while as I went to various booths trying to get checked in, but I laughed it off and got it straightened out.

Okay, to race day:

As mentioned earlier, race morning was cold and windy! I get everything set up and we work our way down to the water about 15-minutes before the race is supposed to start (7:00 am). Then, with just a few minutes before the pros are to go off they make an announcement that they are going to have to cancel the swim because of the very unsafe conditions. The Weather Channel said the swells were 5-6 feet. ARGH! With swimming being one of my strengths, that would make it a lot harder for me to qualify for Kona if I have a good day. Plus, I was looking forward to the swim because the rough water and water temps at 77 degrees, according to the web, would have really suited me. Oh well, take what the day gives you right?

So, now we have to go back to our bikes and get ready to do a time-trial start with our bikes. The pros start at 8:00, and then they start the age-groupers two at a time every several seconds. With thousands of athletes signed up, there are a LOT of people to go through. I didn't get to go until 8:48 and had to stand around literally shivering in the cold. Luckily, I had put two plastic bags against my chest and under my suit to help keep me warm and I had arm-warmers and pretty heavy gloves.

Once we get started, I immediately feel how tough the day is going to be; starting with some scary cross winds to get out of town that had me leaning sideways and getting pushed across the road, then turning straight into the headwinds for 20 miles. I managed this section well, keeping myself in check and making sure I kept a nice smooth cadence, but it was still very difficult pushing into steady winds that strong. For the rest of the course, you had a lot of cross winds and more sections straight into the wind, but you had to keep thinking that once you get to about mile 82 the wind would be mostly at your back except for one 5-mile stint. I knew I was doing okay and had worked my way up toward the front while conserving my energy as best I could. Even still, by mile 60-65 I admit that my mind was toying with me and I just wanted to be off the bike. However, I stuck it out and around mile 75 I started to pick it up as planned and started to pass some of the few that had passed me while they were working too hard into the wind.

Then, I noticed that something didn't feel right with the bike. Is it my tire? Just as that's going through my head, I hit a turn and crash hard as my tire rolls. I wasn't sure what had happened, though. I got back up, fixed my bike, and started to roll again trying to not look at the damage to myself. Obviously, I only made it a short way before realizing that my tire was flat. So, I stop on the side of the road to fix it. This is where it gets even more fun. My bike is off of the road and I have one leg on the white line on the side of the road as I put the Pit Stop onto my tire valve. All of a sudden, some idiot who wasn't paying any attention runs right into my ankle with his pedal going probably 25 mph! It was excruciating and immediately sent white hot pain up my leg. At first I thought for sure it was broken, plus when he hit me it broke my Pit Stop into three pieces, so I had to hope I was able to put enough in the tire. I limped back onto the road and gingerly got back onto the bike. My ankle hurt really badly, but I was able to ride as long as I didn't push too hard with that leg.

THEN, the tire goes flat AGAIN! At this point, I didn't have any more repair stuff and didn't want to get off of my bike because I didn't even know if I'd be able to get back on. So, I sat up, slowed way down and rode the final 13 miles of the Ironman on a flat tire. I had to basically walk around the turns to keep myself upright and avoid crashing again. What made it worse, in a way, was that this was on the section with a major, crazy fast, tail wind, and I couldn't take advantage of it. Finally hitting T2, I see Monette and Katie and stop on the road to tell them that I doubt that I'm going to be able to run, but head into the changing tent to take a look at things.

In the changing tent, I take off my sock and see that my ankle is grotesquely swollen, so the guy helping me calls for the medics. When they get there, they inform me that they can't take me and treat me unless I'm willing to abandon the race. UGH! I ask for them to just take a look and they say that nothing looks broken and they think it's a deep bone bruise. They ask me to walk around on it and I say that it feels okay as long as I keep my foot straight. The medic kindly walks me out of transition to the start of the run to make sure I'm okay, but I grit my teeth and go, ignoring the pain as best I can.

If you've ever tried to ride on a flat, it saps your energy pretty quickly, not that I ever recommend trying that. So, between my legs being way more tired than I'd like and the pains from the crashes, it was very tough mentally. I tried to think about keeping a steady quick turnover and not pushing too hard. That worked for about 5-6 miles probably, but my body was sending me all kinds of signals along the way that it was exhausted. By mile 8-9 I, once again, didn't know how I was going to get through the race. Running into Monette and Katie around mile 11 was nice as I was just about to start walking. I told them that it may take me a while, but I was going to try to get through it.

Man, those miles seemed to keep getting longer and longer. By mile 14, I started to walk for probably 30-seconds or so at the aid stations and wogging (a mix between walking and jogging) between. It was to the point where if I came up on someone that I could pass but was running close to my pace, I would just stay behind them and keep it easy rather than extend myself. At that point, I really just wanted to finish and it took every bit of my will power to keep going. At the same time, I was enjoying all of the people cheering for me as AlvaroJavier!

But, I did keep going. Coming into the last stretch, it was nice to run into a friend from Chapel Hill. While we didn't talk a whole lot, it still really helps to see a friendly face out there. I've rarely been so happy to see the finish line and all of the support after such a difficult day; finishing on a much different note than expected, but just as happy in a different kind of way. I was still surprised at how fast both my bike and runs were, relatively, and how I placed given how the day unfolded. I guess it maybe showed 'what could have been', but I won't play that game and learned a lot more, both about racing and myself, than on a perfect day. After crossing the finish line, they wanted to clean my wounds and the peroxide scrubs just added to the fun! And, having pushed past new limits, I did throw up a couple of times over the next hour. But, I survived, and the Pizza, breadsticks, and ice cream that Monette and Katie were kind enough to get really hit the spot.

So, there you have it, if you've read this far. After a good year of racing, my season ended on a memorable one. D.W.

Triathlon de Nice

My 2014 season ended with a memorable race too. We were spending the Fall semester living on the French Riviera (tough life!) and we decided to enter the Triathlon de Nice at the end of September, which was also serving as the French National Olympic-Distance Championships. It was an incredible experience, but I can't say that Nice was especially "nice" to me. It would not qualify as a complete "disaster," but I had one of the most frustrating and disappointing races of my life.

The race starts out on the beach in Nice, with a 1.5K swim in the beautiful azure-blue Mediterranean Sea. You then do a very long T1 along the cement beach promenade, followed by a 40K bike that features a climb of the Col d'Eze, a relentless 10K ascent that averages about a 6% grade. This climb is a fixture in the annual Paris-Nice bicycle classic done by the top professional cyclists, and it has also been part of the route in the Tour de France a few times. It's stunningly scenic, so it's worth the trip, but it also has a wicked descent, filled with sharp turns, potholes, and crazy French cyclists descending at 40 miles per hour. Once you make it back to transition after finishing the bike by riding through a long, dark, scary tunnel, you go back on to the totally-flat promenade for two

5K loops, which unfortunately were in a blazing hot sun and with only a single water stop on each loop.

I knew it was going to be a tough day when I saw how few porta-johns they had and how long the lines were for them. I managed to do my business early enough – although ideally I would have wanted to use them again right before the race started – and then I had to deal with the crowds at the swim start and swim itself. They only had two waves, each with about 800 people in them and only three minutes apart. The first wave was for people who belonged to French triathlon clubs, who were the only people eligible for the national championship awards. The second wave of another 800 people was for the "open" category, or for all non-club French citizens as well as foreigners. Well finding a place to enter the water with this horde of people was challenging, but what was even more daunting was finding a way to swim with this crowd without getting kicked, pulled, pushed, scratched, and nearly drowned. It was impossible! I spent the entire 1500 meters tangled up with other people, rarely able to take a stroke without catching someone else's arm, leg, foot, or head.

Somehow I made it to the swim exit in a pretty good time, which I attribute to either the course being short or to the fact that I was carried along by a huge 1600-person draft. However, then I had to figure out how to get out of the water without beating up my feet too much, since the beach had no sand at all and consisted of stones and boulders, many of which were sharp. Well I failed at this and cut up one of my toes pretty badly, making the long run on cement in T1 more difficult (as well as the subsequent 10K run). I also had a lot of trouble getting out of my wetsuit with the sore, bleeding toe.

Nevertheless, I made it on to my bike in the top-third of the field, kept up a pretty good pace for the first 5K until we hit the big climb, and then things ground to a halt. I kept climbing, but virtually half the field passed me on the uphill and I felt like I was taking forever. Indeed, it took me longer to do the climb during the race than it had in a practice climb I had done a week earlier. I attribute my slowness to several factors: 1) I was worn out from

the swim and T1, 2) I didn't want to push too hard and wanted to save a little energy for the run, 3) I was riding a bike with gearing that wasn't well-suited for the climb and had to power my way up more than spin my way up, and 4) I just couldn't keep up with all those French cyclists who climb hills like that all the time.

The descent was really scary, with all the slow swimmers trying to make up lost time by flying down the hills with reckless abandon. I rode my brakes for most of it, becoming an obstacle for these folks, and I also hit several bad bumps and potholes. One of the bumps loosened my saddle and made it tilt downward for the rest of the ride, slowing me down further and giving me a sore butt to add to my sore toe.

Dismounting at T2, I was frustrated and wanted to call it a day. Yet, I knew Shelly was probably ahead of me (I saw her from a distance in T1) and I wanted to at least greet her on the run so she wouldn't worry that something had happened to me in all that chaos.

So with a sore toe, sore butt, tired legs, and limited hydration possibilities (but with plenty of Gu), I trudged on and finished both loops of the run as one of the last finishers. I was able to greet Shelly during the first loop, and she was a few minutes ahead of me and looked great. I never saw her on the second loop because she opted to drop out after 5K to save a bad knee from further stress, She was happy with what she accomplished and very upbeat as she greeted me at the finish line. I was pretty bummed out, but that dissipated rapidly as we went to a local patisserie to get some chocolate-almond croissants to recover (not recommended!). Admittedly, those weren't my first croissants of our French sabbatical – I had been eating them non-stop for the two weeks prior to the race (and for the rest of our three-month stay). I suspect all those croissants didn't help my hill climbing or race performance very much! P.B.

The Rules Are The Rules

A friend and former teammate found out the hard way that it pays to make sure you know the rules and let others know them as well.

He was doing the famous Eagleman Triathlon and having a fantastic day. In fact, he was the top amateur finisher overall! Unfortunately for him, a buddy of his made a mistake that cost my friend the title and Kona qualification. His friend was video taping him during the run, and started to run in front and then beside him for a little ways to capture some good footage during his amazing race. However, there also happened to be an official right there and they disqualified him for outside assistance/pacing! How a guy running while trying to do video-taping is supposedly pacing the fastest guy on the course, I have yet to figure out. But, he handled it with grace, much more so than anyone else I know would have done. He admitted that it happened and moved on to his post race beverages. Definitely a learning experience, though! D.W.

Nap Time

When I was working on my master's degree in exercise physiology, a classmate and good friend of mine told me that it was on his bucket list to do an Ironman before he turned 30. Of course, I thought it was great and encouraged him to do it. A short while later, he comes up to me saying, "Okay, I've signed up for Ironman Florida. Now you've got to teach me how to swim." I laughed, thinking he was exaggerating, but told him I'd be happy to help build his swimming up for the Ironman. Therefore, we go to the pool so that I can give him a few pointers and I ask him to warm up. He looks at me funny, but jumps in and starts swimming. However, after one 25 yard length, he gets out gasping and pale from the effort! Uh oh, the Ironman is ten months away. That initially sounded like more than enough time, but now...

Well, he put in a lot of work and showed up on race day ready to give it a try. A testament to his desire and fortitude, he did finish the swim with plenty of time to spare to avoid the cut-off. Don't get me wrong, it was exhausting for him, but he did it. He spent over 15 minutes in transition trying to recover, but then did head out on his bike. Being a very laid back guy, he wanted to finish, but have fun along the way and not stress too much. So, as he approached the special needs hand-off about half way through the bike, he had no qualms about saying he was getting tired, laying down in the grass, and taking a fifteen minute nap!

He did fine the rest of the race, even helping another classmate get through the run, and finishing with a lot of time to spare. But, it sure made for an interesting experience all the way around. D.W.

What Happened to My Transition Space?

A friend of ours was excited to have qualified for the Olympic Distance National Championships in Milwaukee in 2014. She was relatively new to triathlon and was eager to test herself against the top athletes in the country. However, one problem after another materialized during her trip and it proved to be a discouraging and financially expensive experience.

To start out, she made hotel reservations too late and had to stay at an expensive place that was fairly far away from the race venue. To top that off, when she went to do packet pick-up and a practice swim the day before the race, she parked her rental car in a spot she thought was legal but later discovered that she received a several-hundred dollar parking ticket. She also had to spend a lot of money on a new wetsuit, after discovering that her old one was ripped and not up to the task of keeping her fast and streamlined in the water.

On race day, new problems emerged. Back home, her teenaged daughter went missing on that day, deciding not to let her father (our friend's ex-husband), with whom she was staying, know that she went camping with her boyfriend on the beach. It took hours of phone calls to finally locate her (and she was fine), which was an unneeded and costly distraction. When the race started, her swim went fine, but she ran out of fluids on the bike and got pretty dehydrated, which slowed down her run tremendously. But what affected her run even more was a big surprise in T2. When she got to where her transition space was supposed to be for racking her bike, she couldn't find it! Someone had knocked down the entire section and the bikes that had been racked already as well as everyone's shoes, wetsuits, race belts, helmets, and everything else were all jumbled together in one big pile. It took over 10 minutes to separate everything out and find her running shoes and race belt. There was nothing she could do and no way for the race-timing folks to make adjustments for this.

I'm sure she learned a lot about pre-race planning, travel, set-up, and nutrition from this experience, and the next time she goes to Nationals she will do much better. P.B.

Clients' Questions

I've learned to never be surprised by what I see and the questions some people will ask after being a coach for over 15 years. Quite a few are even too graphic to put down here, such as ideas on how to avoid painful delicate areas. I'll let you use you're imagination on that one. I've been asked to look at things I didn't want to see and consider things I didn't want to have in my head. At one swim practice, a woman told me she was having an issue with her menstruation and to let her know if I noticed anything while she was swimming. Um, no, if that's the case you shouldn't be getting in! At another practice, we were practicing dive starts and one guy's suit literally split and fell apart as soon as he bent over. Many people have asked advice on how to urinate while racing, to the point where we often just discuss that now before people have the chance to bring it up. Of course, I've also been asked about going #2 in the water. Another thing I don't want to think about. The list can go on and on, but I'm sure you get the picture, whether you wanted to or not. Don't be afraid to ask a coach or expert your questions no matter how odd they may seem. If they've been around, they've likely heard it, seen it, or at least experienced something similar. D.W.

Injury Prone

As you've seen, I've found various and sundry methods of getting injured. Here are a few more that may keep you from doing anything to imitate me.

It's hard to get injured in the pool, right? I've broken a toe by accidentally kicking a rung of a ladder. I've also had my hands slip while doing muscle-ups (an exercise where you pull yourself *up on the edge of the deck and back down) causing me to crash my chin down on the edge of the deck and smashing my teeth. Even as I write this, I'm in a brace with ligament damage to my thumb because I smacked hands with Monette during a workout while she was wearing hand paddles.*

I had no choice but to buy my first triathlon bike because I tried out a nice used bike but had never used clipless pedals before. I proceeded to crash four separate times on that ride. Needless to say, there was no way I was comfortable not buying it after scratching it up like that! One time when I was in college, I came up to a busy intersection with a McDonalds on the corner. I decided to cut into the parking lot and just had to jump a little curb, not even a couple of inches probably. I'm sure you can guess by now that I didn't make it and ended up flipping over my bike in a pretty spectacular fall. Being in a college town, the people in the cars weren't worried if I was alright. No, instead they started honking their horns and cheering!

I've also broken a rib while laughing in the finish chute after a big race, crashed over wet railroad tracks, and had a 25 pound weight fall on my head in the gym, just to name a few. D.W.

Foreign Affairs

One more personal injury story needs it's own title. This one happened in Cozumel, but not actually at the Ironman itself. It's pertinent because it shows that you have to be a little careful if you do get in an accident in some places. Monette and I rented a moped the day after the Ironman to tour around the island. Things were going great and we had a ton of fun, until the last turn that we had to make right on the busiest intersection downtown. I misjudged the turn and crashed the moped causing Monette to fall heavily on top of me. There just happened to be a cop that I fell directly in front of and he ran over to tell me that: "I've called an ambulance, that sounded bad." Monette's reaction was priceless. She started saying that we shouldn't go to the hospital if we really didn't have to. "What's hurting?" I told her that I couldn't move my arm and my shoulder really hurt. She proceeds to start looking around and saying that she's sure someone there would be able to pop in a dislocated shoulder! I told her that if someone tried to touch my shoulder I'd punch them!

The ambulance showed up and took me to a clinic with an accordion door entrance. The doctors spoke very little English and it took a long time to get things going. They eventually told me that they thought I probably broke something and wanted to take an x-ray. They asked me to stand up and follow a guy into the next room. Once there, they stand me straight and a guy runs in holding a film in front of me as they take the x-ray! No protection or anything. Then, they say that the first one turned out fuzzy and they needed to take it again. The same procedure took place again. Who knows how much radiation I got that day, let alone the guy who had to hold the film?

Then, a little while later they say that they think it is broken but have to call in a specialist. Meanwhile, they stick the x-ray above my bed as we wait another hour for the specialist to show up. After he gets there he looks at the x-ray, comes over to us clapping his hands together, then happily tells us that he sees nothing wrong. Monette gaped at him, then pointed at the x-ray and asked, "Then, what's this?" My scapula was badly broken and looked like a V. He just looked at us and said, "Oh! It's in your back, I thought it was your shoulder that hurt." I politely asked for some pain meds and a sling to hold things together until I could get home. Of course, our connecting flight got delayed and we ended having to stay overnight in Texas, which was a very, very uncomfortable night, but we got through it and called my orthopedist, who I practically had on speed dial by this point, as soon as I got home. D.W.

Now, go out and enjoy your training and racing while making your own funny experiences, trying to avoid some of the mistakes and blunders that we've shared. Good luck, have fun, and we hope to see you at a triathlon in the near future – and we'd love to hear the crazy experiences you've had!

ABOUT THE AUTHORS

Paul N. Bloom and David K. Williams are USA Triathlon Certified Coaches with Triangle Multisport in Chapel Hill, North Carolina, a group founded in 2000 by Dave and his wife, Monette (see www.trianglemultisport.com). Both have numerous coaching certifications, with Dave having worked with hundreds of athletes at all levels, including many professional and elite competitors. Dave holds a master's in exercise physiology and an MBA, both from the University of North Carolina. He has also competed successfully himself as both an elite and age-group triathlete, with numerous podium finishes in races of all distances, including Ironman. Prior to moving into coaching a few years ago, Paul had an award-winning career as a business-school professor at three Universities (Maryland, North Carolina at Chapel Hill, and Duke). He has an MBA from the University of Pennsylvania and a Ph.D. from Northwestern University. He has competed successfully in age-group triathlon and duathlon competitions all over the world for more than a decade.

Colleagues, but also rivals, Dave is the head coach of the UNC Triathlon Club, while Paul serves as assistant coach of the Duke Triathlon Club.

Paul can be reached at paulnbloom@gmail.com and Dave can be reached at trimultisport@yahoo.com.

The cartoons were created by John Holladay from Martha's Vineyard, MA. He can be reached at johnsholladay@hotmail.com.

Made in the USA
Charleston, SC
08 October 2015